Overcomer

Overcomer

Stephen Kaung

www.christiantestimonyministry.com

ISBN: 978-1-942521-70-9

Available from:

Christian Testimony Ministry
4424 Huguenot Road
Richmond, Virginia 23235

www.christiantestimonyministry.com

Printed in USA

Contents

1—Christ the Overcomer   7

2—The Call to Overcome   31

3—The Making of Overcomers   53

4—The Task of Overcomers   77

5—The Overcomers and the Church   99

These messages on the theme Overcomer were given in July 1969 at a conference in Wabanna, Maryland. The other two speakers at the conference were T. Austin-Sparks and Devern Fromke. This last call to the churches is still His call today. Though Stephen Kaung shared this over 50 years ago, "he that has an ear" will "hear what the Spirit is speaking to the churches" today.

Unless otherwise indicated,
Scripture quotations are from
The New Translation by J. N. Darby

1—Christ the Overcomer

Our heavenly Father, Thou does know the desire of our hearts. We ask of Thee only one thing and that is Thou will reveal Thy Son in us more and fuller. We want not only to see Him, but we want to be filled by Him. We do pray that as we together wait in Thy presence that it would be Thy pleasure to do this very thing to Thy people. Lord, our heart is that Christ may be exalted, that He truly may be all and in all, that His love may fill our hearts, that we may be unto the praise of His glory. Oh Lord, we ask at this moment that Thou will deliver us from thinking of ourselves, and we pray that we may think only of Thy Son, our Lord Jesus Christ. We do commit this hour into Thy hand. We ask that if it should please Thee that Thou will speak through Thy Word to us, and Thou will do Thy work tonight as Thou has been doing since we began to meet. We do praise and worship Thee together. In the name of our Lord Jesus and for His glory. Amen.

I believe all of you brothers and sisters agree with me that even though we have met just a few times, yet I feel that my heart is very full. I do thank the Lord that we do not need to wait until the end of our time together to begin to realize what He means to us. I do praise the Lord that we may experience what He means to us even from the very beginning because He is the first and we believe He is also the last.

Several months ago as I was thinking of this time that we would have together, I was before the Lord wondering what He would have us to consider together before Him, and just one word came to me. During the past few months I will say that in the very beginning I did not put too much thought on that one word, although it has been with me. But I have not really meditated upon it until the Lord set me aside, and it was during that time it began to become stronger and stronger in me. Many times I asked the Lord if this is what He wanted to speak through this little instrument for this time, and somehow I feel this is what the Lord wants to say. Therefore, I hope that during our times together, if the Lord wills, that we will consider together this one word. I do not know if this has been the exercise of your hearts during the past year or so, but that one word is very simple. If I mention it you will know it already, and that is the word *overcomer*.

> Revelation 5:1-14—And I saw on the right hand of him that sat upon the throne a book, written within and on the back, sealed with seven seals. And I saw a strong angel proclaiming with a loud voice, Who is worthy to open the book, and to break its seals? And no one was able in the heaven, or upon the earth, or underneath the

earth, to open the book, or to regard it. And I wept much because no one had been found worthy to open the book nor to regard it. And one of the elders says to me, Do not weep. Behold, the lion which is of the tribe of Juda, the root of David, has overcome so as to open the book, and its seven seals.

And I saw in the midst of the throne and of the four living creatures, and in the midst of the elders, a Lamb standing, as slain, having seven horns and seven eyes, which are the seven Spirits of God which are sent into all the earth: and it came and took it out of the right hand of him that sat upon the throne. And when it took the book, the four living creatures and the twenty-four elders fell before the Lamb, having each a harp and golden bowls full of incense, which are the prayers of the saints. And they sing a new song, saying, Thou art worthy to take the book, and to open its seals; because thou hast been slain, and hast redeemed to God, by thy blood, out of every tribe, and tongue and people, and nation, and made them to our God kings and priests; and they shall reign over the earth.

And I saw, and I heard the voice of many angels around the throne and the living creatures and the elders; and their number was ten thousands ten thousands and thousands of thousands; saying with a loud voice, Worthy is the Lamb that has been slain, to receive power, and riches, and wisdom, and strength, and honour, and glory, and blessing. And every creature which is in the heaven and upon the earth and under the earth, and those that are upon the sea, and all things in them, heard I saying, To him that sits upon the throne, and to the Lamb, blessing, and honour, and glory, and might, to the ages of ages. And the four living creatures said, Amen; and the elders fell down and did homage.

The Scene of Redemption

We have a very wonderful chapter before us of a glorious scene in heaven. I believe most people know that this is a scene of the glory of redemption. Chapter 4 of the book of Revelation tells us of the glory of creation. Chapter 4:11 says, "Thou art worthy, O our Lord and our God, to receive glory and honour and power; for thou hast created all things, and for thy will they were, and they have been created." So this tells us of the glory of creation or we may say the glory of the Creator. What a glorious scene we see in chapter 4!

Following that we have this fifth chapter before us which is the glory of redemption because mentioned here is this, "Thou art worthy to take the book, and to open its seals; because thou hast been slain, and hast redeemed to God, by thy blood, out of every tribe, and tongue, and people, and nation, and made them to our God kings and priest; and they shall reign over the earth" (vv. 9-10).

Again he says, "Worthy is the Lamb that has been slain, to receive power, and riches, and wisdom, and strength, and honour, and glory, and blessing" (v. 12).

This is the song of redemption; it is the glory of the Redeemer. Whether you believe that this is also the theme of the ascension of our Lord, whether you believe that this happens at the time of our Lord's ascension or not, I think this is not of great importance because redemption is eternal. The glory of redemption is eternal. But personally I feel that this describes the scene at the ascension of our Lord Jesus. As He ascended up to heaven, this glorious scene is opened to us.

For the sake of having some background in which we desire to fellowship, I am afraid that we will have to get into a little interpretation. Now this is something I would like to avoid very much because we know that people have interpreted especially the book of Revelation in so many different ways, and every interpreter feels that his is *the* interpretation. So I am very much afraid to offer you another interpretation or to follow the interpretation of any person. So I do hope that you will bear with me if I have to do a little interpretation, and if you do not agree with me I am perfectly happy with that. I certainly do not want to force you into my interpretation.

I remember some years ago when I was in South America, I met a servant of the Lord, and we began to have some time together. He began to press me concerning certain passages in the Scriptures. He wanted me to tell him how I felt about them or my understanding of these passages. I try my best to avoid such things, but he pressed me and I had no way out. I knew what he was after, and he just cornered me and would not let me off. So I felt that I had to say something. So I told him what I personally believed, but that I am willing to change my interpretation if I find out that it is not the most satisfactory one. Even though I tried to tell him in this way he replied by saying that I did not believe in the Bible. The reason was that it so happened my interpretation was different from his on these passages. So I tried to tell my brother that I do believe the Bible. We may differ in interpretation, but certainly we believe the Bible. However, his mind was made up. So I believe that you will not treat me this way because if you do I would rather just sit down.

For the sake of giving some background I am afraid I will have to do a little interpretation, and as I said, if you do not agree with it I am perfectly happy. You can keep on interpreting it in the way that you used to. The important thing is not the interpretation; the important thing is that which we are driving at. If we can really see what we are driving at then you can forget about the interpretation.

A Glorious Scene in Heaven

We are before this glorious scene in heaven, and I think there was a great suspense. As you come to this chapter I believe you should hold your breath because here is One who is sitting on the throne and in His hand was a book. However, it was a sealed book, and a proclamation went forth: "Who is worthy to take the book from the hand of the One who sits upon the throne to open it and read it?" But after the mighty angel had made this proclamation, there was no response for a time. There was no response in heaven, no response on earth, no response anywhere in the universe. I believe that if you were there (and we should be there), there would be great suspense. You do not know what will happen, and if you really knew what it meant you would weep as much as the apostle John. When the apostle John waited and waited and there was no answer, no response, he wept much. Why? Because he knew so much was involved. It was not just a matter of a person or a few people; it was a matter that concerns the eternal purpose of God. He wept because if there was no response then everything is really finished.

Then you will remember that an elder comforted him and said, "Weep not; behold the Lion of the tribe of Judah, the root of David has overcome, and because He has overcome therefore He is worthy to take the book, open it, and make it known." Now what is that book? That is where the interpretation comes in. I personally believe, and I know many believe the same way, that this is the title deed of the earth. This book tells us of the right of God over His created earth. You know that God created the heavens and the earth. He was not only the Creator of the universe; He was also the Owner of the universe. He had never given up His ownership, though He often gave up stewardship. But the ownership is ever in His hand.

God gave the Stewardship of the Earth to an Archangel

Once upon a time, if our understanding of the Scripture is correct, God seemed to give the universe up to an archangel to be under his rulership, under his stewardship. This archangel was to rule the earth for the glory of God. But somehow unrighteousness was found in this archangel, and the whole earth entered into emptiness and became void.

Man was Given Dominion Over the Earth

Then God created man, but before He created man He first made the earth habitable. I think one thing we should know; God never works along a mechanical line. God is well able to restore the earth mechanically, physically, and He did to a certain degree. But God's way is always along a spiritual and moral principle. He did restore the earth out of ruin and made it habitable, but that does not mean God has restored the earth. The restoration waits upon something that runs along a spiritual and moral line, and that is the reason why God created man. God created a being a little lower than angels, and with that being He is going to subdue and restore the earth morally and spiritually into the very plan and thought of God. He did restore the earth physically, but that was only a preparation. He created man with the hope that through man the whole earth, all the created things will be restored unto God to the praise of His glory. In other words, when man was created, you remember he was created in the image of God, and he was given dominion over the earth. He was created in the image of God that he might communicate with God, that he might receive God into himself, and that he might know God and His way. He was given dominion, power, and authority over the created things, and we know all these are for the purpose of bringing the earth back to God's intended purpose.

Dear brothers and sisters, from here we know of one thing; man is created with the purpose of being an overcomer. God does not create man to be defeated. God created man with a purpose that through him the adversary of God would be defeated.

In other words, man is created with the purpose of being an overcomer. It is only when man overcomes that God's purpose will be fulfilled, and God has made every provision for man to be an overcomer. He is created in the image of God so that he may overcome. He is given dominion so that he may overcome. He is given every opportunity, every possibility of overcoming the adversary, and yet we know Adam was defeated. In other words, the stewardship of man failed, but that does not mean that the ownership of God is jeopardized because in the hand of the One who sits upon the throne is the book. God still holds the ownership of this earth and all the created things, but He is waiting for that man, the overcomer, to restore the earth and to bring everything back to the purpose of God.

About three thousand years later David, by the Holy Spirit, began to mention this: "What is man that thou art mindful of him? and the son of man, thou visitest him? Thou hast made him a little lower than the angels, and hast crowned him with glory and splendour. Thou hast made him to rule over the works of thy hands; thou hast put everything under his feet: sheep and oxen, all of them, and also the beasts of the field; the fowl of the heavens, and the fishes of the sea, whatever passeth through the paths of the seas" (Psalm 8:4-8).

God had not given up His thought. Here He is still speaking of man. "What is man that thou art mindful of him and the son of man that thou visitest him? Thou hast made him a little inferior, a little lower than angels, but has crowned him with glory and splendor and has given him dominion over all the created things." The first man had failed, but God had not given up the concept of the man, the overcomer. So in one sense, through David, God reassured us that He had not changed His mind. He was still looking for the man, the overcomer. On the other hand, through the prophet David He foretells that one day the Man of God's heart will come, and when He comes, God's purpose shall be fulfilled.

Another thousand years went by and in Hebrews 2:6-10 it says, "What is man, that thou rememberest him, or son of man that thou visitest him? Thou hast made him some little inferior to the angels; thou hast crowned him with glory and honour, and hast set him over the works of thy hands; thou hast subjected all things under his feet. For in subjecting all things to him, he has left nothing unsubject to him. But now we see not yet all things subjected to him, but we see Jesus, who was made some little inferior to angels on account of the suffering of death, crowned with glory and honour; so that by the grace of God he should taste death for every thing. For it became him, for whom are all things, and by whom are all things, in bringing many sons to glory, to make perfect the leader of their salvation through sufferings."

God Finds His Man, the Overcomer

Four thousand years later in Christ Jesus God finally found His Man, and here it is connected with Revelation chapter 5 in which you find this Man, the Overcomer. He ascended on high and there He was given this book to open and to make it known. In other words, He alone is worthy to execute the plan of God concerning the earth and, of course, all created beings. In this chapter 5 of Revelation we find the glory of the Redeemer and Christ the Overcomer.

Very often when we think of the word overcomer, we start with ourselves. How can I be an overcomer? How can I overcome? So we try to overcome. I think the very thought of an overcomer is too self-centered, and probably this is the reason why we are overcome instead of overcoming. The right concept of overcomer in the Bible must begin with Him. First, we must have a vision of Him, of Christ, the Overcomer. Unless we know Christ as *the* Overcomer we will never overcome. Our whole possibility of being an overcomer rests upon Him, *the* Overcomer. So I do look to the Lord that we not start with ourselves because if we do we will also end in ourselves. We will never get out of ourselves. I believe that the Lord wants us to see Him, to behold Him. The word says, "Behold!" There is no overcomer except One. Who is worthy? No one is worthy but He. Behold the Man, the Overcomer!

The Lion and the Lamb

In the book of Revelation, very often it is written in symbolic terms. In chapter 5 you find that the elder is comforting the weeping apostle saying, "Weep not; it is not as hopeless as you think." Actually it is very hopeful. Behold the Lion of the tribe of Judah, the root of David. Of course, you are not looking for a real lion; it is a figurative way of speaking. Behold the Lion of the tribe of Judah. This lion character, this lion feature of Christ describes to us an inward character, and with this character He overcomes. Then later on as he tries to look for the Lion he saw a Lamb. So if you are really looking for a Lion you will not find it because you will see a Lamb. Again, we will say this lamb is symbolic, representative. It reveals a lamb character. Our Lord Jesus is *the* Overcomer and He overcomes on the basis of these two characters. How does He overcome? He overcomes as a Lion and He overcomes as a Lamb. In these two features He accomplishes victory.

The Lion Character

Let us look a little bit into these two features, first a lion. Now when you see a lion or when you hear the word lion, what is the impression that comes to you? When you think of a lion, immediately you realize that a lion is the king of the beasts. He is majestic, powerful, full of strength, bold, fearless, accepts every challenge, never retreats. All these thoughts will come to you. Our Lord Jesus is the Lion of the tribe of Judah. As we read the four gospels we will see in the life of our Lord Jesus a lion character. First of all, there is that singleness of purpose, that utter devotedness unto the Father. There is no looking to the right or to the left or even looking backward, but our Lord Jesus set His face like flint. He is like a lion; He never goes back. He sets His heart upon the will of the Father and there He goes. There is no deviation; there is no compromise. There is only that singleness of heart and purpose and determination. There is no fear. That is the lion character.

When our Lord Jesus was twelve, He reached the age of being a son of the law, and He went with His earthly parents to Jerusalem, and He tarried there. Finally, they found Him in the temple asking questions and answering them. When His earthly parents asked Him, "Why, child, do You treat us this way?" Our Lord Jesus said, "Should I not be occupied with My Father's business?" This happened when He was twelve, and you may say this is the age of accountability. He was certainly accountable before the God, and His heart was set upon the Father.

When He was thirty, John the Baptist was baptizing the people, and He asked to be baptized. John hesitated and said, "I should be baptized by You, and do You come to me to be baptized?" But the Lord Jesus said, "Suffer it; it is for righteousness." There He offered Himself as a sacrifice for the sins of this world. Ever since that time our Lord Jesus had His heart set upon the Father. When He was in the wilderness, He was tempted for forty days and forty nights. Oh, how Satan tried to draw Him out, tried to make Him claim who He was, which was His rightful claim because He is the Son of God. "If you are the Son of God, turn these stones into bread." He is the Son of God, and He certainly could have turned those stones into bread, but the Lord Jesus refused him, and said, "Man does not live by bread alone but by every word that proceeds from the mouth of God."

Throughout His life there was that singleness of purpose, that utter devotedness unto the Father. He said, "Your time is always ready, but my time is not yet come. You can do anything you like but I cannot. I speak because My Father has spoken. I do it because I have seen Him do it." Our Lord Jesus had committed Himself fully to the Father, and He walked straight without any deviation. Even in the garden of Gethsemane His prayer was "Not My will but Thy will be done." The first feature of a lion character is His steadfastness of spirit, determination of heart, singleness of mind, wholly committed and devoted to the Father. Oh, there is such a holy boldness in our Lord Jesus. When you read the four gospels, you find that our Lord Jesus was not afraid to uncover the mask of the Pharisees. He was not afraid to tear off the pretension of traditionalism. He was bold as a lion, and He overcame. He overcame because He is the Lion of the tribe of Judah.

We Overcome Through Union with Christ

Of course, we know one thing which is most basic, if you want to overcome anything, the first thing is you must overcome yourself. If you have not overcome yourself, you will not be able to overcome anything, however small that thing may be. We always try to overcome this thing and that thing. If you start that way you will discover that even though that thing is a very small thing, it overcomes you. If you want to be an overcomer the first thing is to overcome yourself.

Look at our Lord Jesus. How He denied Himself completely—His holy self. His self is not like our self. There is no good in our self, in our flesh, but His is different. His is a holy self, and yet in the life of our Lord Jesus He completely denied Himself. He had full control over Himself. Never for a moment did He give in to Himself, to His holy self, we must say. Now it is almost beyond our understanding because we do not have this experience of a holy self. But our Lord Jesus is so holy and blameless and spotless, yet He said, "Not my will but Thy will be done." He had full control over His self, and because He had overcome His self so completely He could overcome that which was around Him.

Towards the end of His life He said, "You will have tribulation in this world, but you do not need to be afraid for I have overcome the world." He was in the world, but He was not of the world. The world tried to get into Him. The world tried its best to get into Him, but towards the end, the world realized they had to get Him out because He would never let the world in. He had overcome the world. Do not think that overcoming the world is just overcoming this thing or that thing, do not go to this place or to that place, give up this thing or that thing, and that is overcoming the world. Not at all. It may be included, but overcoming the world is not letting the world have a foothold in your life. That is overcoming the world.

He overcame sin completely. He was tempted in all things just as we are, but without sin. He had overcome sin because of His utter devotedness unto the Father. He overcame the ruler of this world. Even toward the end of His life He said, "The ruler of this world has come but he has no place in me." There was no place, and because of this He was able to spoil the principalities and authorities, and He made a show of them openly because He overcame the ruler of this world.

Then of course He overcame death. The last enemy is death, but here you find He has gone into death. He did not try to avoid death, but He has gone into death. He brought death to death and out He comes in resurrection power.

The life of our Lord Jesus overcomes as a lion. If we want to be overcomers there must be this lion character in us, but we do not have it. You may have a very strong will, and I think it is easier to find strong wills than weak wills. One day a few of us were talking together and one sister said, "Everyone is strong-willed." I agreed with her. I think it is very difficult to find a weak-willed person. We are all weak-willed in certain things, in a certain respect, that is true. But in the core of our will all of us are very strong. Even though we are very strong-willed, yet we do not overcome. This lion character is not in us. But thank God, because Christ is the Lion of the tribe of Judah He has overcome. How do we overcome? By being in union with Him. It is only by our being united with Him in one that His character begins to characterize us. That is how we are brought into overcoming experiences. Do not think that to be an overcomer is just by listening to some overcoming messages or by claiming Romans 6. These may be included, yes, but it is not an outward formula. Christianity is not a system of formulas by which repeating certain magic words you will overcome; that is not Christianity. The only way to overcome is to be united with the Overcomer. It is His life, it is His character that overcomes and nothing else. This is only one side.

The Lamb Character

We find there is another side when the elder said, "Behold the Lion of the tribe of Judah." Well, the apostle John began to open his eyes. You know when you are weeping you do not see very clearly. So he tried to open his weeping eyes and locate the lion, but he could not see the lion. He saw a Lamb slain, standing. You see, all of these are paradoxes because a lion cannot be a lamb nor can a lamb slain stand. But here is a Lamb slain, yet standing with seven horns and seven eyes which are the seven Spirits of God that are sent to all the earth. This is the other side of Christ the Overcomer. There is both the lion side and the lamb side, and naturally, lion and lamb cannot be together. But in the life of our Lord Jesus, on the one side there is the lion character and at the same time there is the lamb character. He overcomes as the lion, and probably we can understand that. But He also overcomes as the lamb which is beyond human reason. And the greatest victory of our Lord Jesus is through this lamb character. He is the Lamb slain from the foundation of the world. In Isaiah 53 when the prophet prophesied about our Lord Jesus he described the lamb character of our Lord. "He was oppressed, and he was afflicted, but he opened not his mouth; he was led as a lamb to the slaughter, and was as a sheep dumb before her shearers, and he opened not his mouth. He was taken from oppression and from judgment; and who shall declare his generation? For he was cut off out of the land of the living; for the transgression of my people was he stricken" (vv. 7-8). He is the Lamb.

He was born in a manager as a little Baby, helpless. We might think that if the Savior of the world should come, He would come forth as a full-grown Man because He would be the symbol of strength. Adam came forth as a full-grown man when he was created, but this full-grown man was a very weak man. Our Lord Jesus came to this earth as a Babe, weak, helpless, and yet the greatest strength was in that Baby. He was brought up in Nazareth. No good thing ever came out of Nazareth. He was like a root out of dry ground. There was no comeliness, no outward beauty to attract our attention. And throughout the life of our Lord Jesus He said, "I am meek and lowly of heart. Take my yoke upon you and learn of me." He was reviled, but He never reviled back. He is a Lamb, humble, meek and lowly. He never tried to hurt anyone. When He was hurt, He never answered back. He was like a lamb led to the place of slaughter and He was silent. He was like a sheep being sheared by the shearers.

All His wool was being sheared off—all His beauty, all His glory. Oh, how people sheared Him, stripped Him, took away everything from Him. He was silent. He was willing to suffer; He was willing to die on the cross. The way of the Lamb is the way of the cross.

The Victory of the Cross

Why is it that God has to use the Lamb slain, the cross to overcome? It is because of the recourse and the consequence of the fall of man. Man fell because of pride, of independence, of self-exaltation. This is the cause of the fall of man. In order to deliver man the cross is the only way; it is where self is denied, is crucified and is taken away. Oh, by being the Lamb of God so meek and lowly, who suffered so much, endured so much in silence and finally died on the cross as the Lamb slain, this is the victory. The greatest victory in the universe is obtained through this Lamb character of our Lord Jesus.

How can we overcome? How can we ever be overcomers? There must be this lamb character in us. Sometimes we are as bold as lions. We devour everything. There is no lamb character in us. Where is the spirit of the Lamb? Where is the spirit of humility? Where is the willingness to suffer in silence? Yes, sometimes we suffer, but the whole world knows about it. We are lacking in our self being taken away. Selflessness comes by way of the cross. We lack this lamb character. Even though we are very bold and sometimes too bold, we do not overcome. There has to be a combination of these two, and no one can put them together. No one can do that; it is only by union with Christ; that is the only way.

So let us remember one thing. God is looking for overcomers. His whole plan rests upon man as overcomer. But to be an overcomer there is only one way, and that is by union with Christ. *That is the only way*. It is only when we are united with Christ, then Christ *the* overcomer begins to characterize us. This lion character and lamb character begin to grow in us, and as Christ is gradually formed in us He receives men as overcomers. So let our eyes be focused upon Him. Do not look at yourselves. If you look at yourselves you will be discouraged, but let our eyes be focused upon Christ and see Him as *the* Overcomer. And the Lamb slain standing is resurrection, with seven horns and seven eyes. Horns speak of power, full of power; eyes speak of discernment, full of wisdom. These are the seven Spirits of God that are sent to all the earth. Why? To overcome. It is no wonder that in this glorious chapter you find the anthem rising up throughout the universe starting with the angels, thousands and thousands, tens of thousands, and they are praising Christ the Redeemer, and there is the response by all the created things ending up with Amen and worship.

Oh, dear brothers and sisters, if only we can see Christ as *the* Overcomer, it will bring us into a worshipping spirit.

Let us pray:

> Our heavenly Father, we pray that we may see Thy Son, behold the Lion, the Lamb slain standing. Oh, we pray that we may see Christ as the Man, the Overcomer in whom all Thy purpose is fulfilled, who is worthy alone to bring Thy purpose into full realization. Oh, how we praise and thank Thee that we are by grace united with Him. His victory is our victory, not only objectively, but because He is our victory, His very life is ours, His very character is ours. Oh, how we praise and thank Thee that Thou has been so gracious to us that we may be a part of Him, of Him who is the overcoming life. Oh, may all the praise and glory and adoration of our hearts be unto God and to the Lamb forever and ever. Amen.

2—The Call to Overcome

May we look to the Lord in prayer:

Oh Lord, we are gathered together in Thy victorious name. Oh, how we praise and thank Thee that we are today in the good of Thy victory, and it is upon this ground that we meet. We praise and thank Thee as the enemy has no place in Thee, he has no place in us. Oh, how we praise and thank Thee because of Thy victory. We claim Thy victory together for tonight that Thy will may be done on earth as it is in heaven, that the enemy shall be defeated, bound and cast out, and Thou shall be exalted and seen and heard and worshipped and loved. Oh Lord, we do commit this time completely into Thy hands. In the name of our Lord Jesus. Amen.

Revelation 1:9-18—I John, your brother and fellow-partaker in the tribulation and kingdom and patience, in Jesus, was in the island called Patmos, for the word of God, and for the testimony of Jesus. I became in the Spirit on the Lord's day, and I heard behind me a great voice as of a trumpet, saying, What thou seest write in a book, and send to the seven assemblies: to Ephesus, and to Smyrna, and to Pergamos, and to Thyatira, and to Sardis, and to Philadelphia, and to Laodicea.

And I turned back to see the voice which spoke with me; and having tuned, I saw seven golden lamps, and in the midst of the seven lamps one like the Son of man, clothed with a garment reaching to the feet, and girt about at the breasts with a golden girdle: his head and hair white like white wool, as snow; and his eyes as a flame of fire; and his feet like fine brass, as burning in a furnace; and his voice as the voice of many waters; and having in his right hand seven stars; and out of his mouth a sharp two-edged sword going forth; and his countenance as the sun shines in its power.

And when I saw him I fell at his feet as dead; and he laid his right hand upon me, saying, Fear not; I am the first and the last, and the living one: and I became dead, and behold, I am living to the ages of ages, and have the keys of death and of hades.

Revelation 2:7, 11, 17, 26; 3:5, 12, 21—He that has an ear, let him hear what the Spirit says to the assemblies. To him that overcomes, I will give to him to eat of the tree of life which is in the paradise of God...He that has an ear, let him hear what the Spirit says to the assemblies. He that overcomes shall in no wise be injured of the second death...He that has an ear, let him hear what the Spirit says to the assemblies. To him that overcomes, to him will I give of the hidden manna, and I will give to him a white stone, and on the stone a new name written, which no one knows but he that receives it…And he that overcomes, and he that keeps unto the end my works, to him will I give authority over the nations, and he shall rule them with an iron rod; as vessels of pottery are they broken in pieces, as I also have received from my Father; and I will give to him the morning star. He that has an ear, let him hear what the Spirit says to the assemblies…he that overcomes, he shall be clothed in white garments, and I will not blot his name out of the book of life, and will confess his name before my Father and before his angels. He that has an ear, let him hear what the Spirit says to the assemblies…He that overcomes, him will I make a pillar in the temple of my God, and he shall go no more at all out; and I will write upon him the name of my God, and the name of the city of my God, the new Jerusalem, which comes down out of heave, from my God, and my new name. He that has an ear, let him hear what the Spirit says to the assemblies…He that overcomes, to him will I give to sit with me in my throne; as I also have overcome, and have sat down with my Father in his throne. He that has an ear, let him hear what the Spirit says to the assemblies.

The Call has Gone Out

We mentioned that there is only One who has overcome, and this is our Lord Jesus. He is *the*

Overcomer, and it is on the basis of this that the call to overcome has gone out. God can never call for overcomers if His Son had not overcome. But after our Lord Jesus overcame then the call is out. The call to overcome is now upon every one of the children of God. According to the order of this book of Revelation it seems as if we are going backward, but as has been said, by going backward we are going onward and fuller.

We considered together the fifth chapter because spiritually speaking this is the foundation of chapters 1-3. It is on the basis of Christ as *the* Overcomer, the basis of His ascension, and the basis of the glory of the Redeemer that we find the first three chapters in the book of Revelation. So spiritually speaking, this will be the right order. In chapter one, of course, we know it is the vision that the apostle John saw on the isle of Patmos. It is a wonderful vision, a glorious vision. It is the vision of the Son of man in the midst of seven golden candlesticks or lampstands. That is the vision.

The Son of Man in the Midst of the Lampstands

Before there is the call to overcome, there is the need of seeing the vision. The vision actually constitutes the call. Where there is no vision, there is no call. It is only when a vision is seen that the call is upon us. Very often we feel that we have not received the call. Why is it that some people have heard the call while others have not? The reason is that some have seen the vision while others have not. So the most important thing is for us to see the vision. Of course, by vision it does not mean that it is something you see with your physical eyes. A vision is an unveiling of the mind of God to our spirit; that is vision.

This vision is of the Son of man who is in the midst of seven golden lampstands. The Son of man is in the foreground, and the seven golden lampstands form the background, and by joining these together you have the perfect vision. In this vision the Son of man is described in detail, but there is no description of the seven golden candlesticks. Why? Because the mind of God is that we may see Christ, the revelation of Jesus Christ. That is what God wants us to see. God wants us to see Christ in the foreground, and of course we know by seeing Him we see the seven golden candlesticks. In other words, the seven golden candlesticks take their character from the Son of man. Therefore, what the Son of man is will be what the seven golden candlesticks are. That is why only the Son of man is described while the seven golden candlesticks are not described at all. By seeing Christ you see the church, but Christ is always in the foreground, and the church is always in the background. The mind of God is that we may see Him, but always with the candlesticks as the background. If we see Him without any background we will not be able to see Him in His fullness. It is like a painting that an artist is going to paint. He may be thinking of painting some trees, but he does not want to just paint the trees without a background because with that background the foreground will stand out. It will be seen more vividly, more distinctly and more clearly.

Now that is the way of God. He does want us to focus our attention upon His Son the Lord Jesus Christ, but in order that we may see Him standing out, He gives us a background which is always the church. We must remember that the church is never in the foreground and Christ in the background. Now if you try to do that then you will see nothing. So here you find the unity between Christ and His church. The church takes its character from Christ; the church uplifts Christ and makes Christ more distinctive. The church *is* the background and the Son of man *is* the foreground.

Here He is described in many features. In the first place He is called the Son of man. We know that this is a title that our Lord Jesus used of Himself while He was on earth. The Son of man—what is the meaning of it? Of course, it means a lot, but we will just say that by being the Son of man it means that He is the beginning of a new mankind. God is forming a new mankind and it is being formed according to Christ, the Son of man. It is the beginning of a new mankind, and it is full of life, full of life.

The Sight of Christ

He is clothed with a garment down to the feet meaning that He is full of righteousness down to the feet. He is girt about at the breast with a golden girdle, full of divine life. And His head and hair are white as white wool, white as snow, and full of wisdom. His eyes are as a flame of fire, full of spiritual discernment, penetrating sight. His feet are like unto burnished brass as if they had been refined in a furnace. A brass that is refined in a furnace shines full of light. "If we walk in the light as He is in the light we have fellowship with one another and the blood of Jesus Christ God's Son cleanses us from all our iniquities" (I John 1:7). His voice is as the voice of many waters, full of strength, powerful. He has in His right hand seven stars, fully responsible. Out of His mouth precedes a sharp two-edged sword, dividing, cutting asunder, purifying. And His countenance is as the sun shining in His strength, full of glory.

Dear brothers and sisters, what we have here is a sight of Christ, the Son over His house, the great High Priest in His true censoring, the King in His own kingdom. That is what we see. We see a sight of Christ and how glorious, magnificent, and majestic Christ is. And we know that as He is so is the church. The seven golden lampstands take their character from the Son of man.

The Vocation in the Church

Following this vision there is the vocation as found in chapters 2 and 3. First there is the vision of Christ in the midst of His church, and secondly there is the vocation of the church. In these two chapters are the seven churches in Asia. Now these seven churches are not hypothetical cases. They are actual churches in the Roman province of Asia at the time of John the apostle, and they really existed at the end of the first century before the last of the twelve apostles passed away.

These seven churches in Asia are represented by the seven golden lampstands, and God chose them at the end of the first century. Why? We know that there were more than seven churches in the Roman province of Asia at that time, but the Holy Spirit just chose these seven because they will give us a full picture of the church of God at that time and even up to now. The condition of the church of God is fully represented by the seven churches in Asia. So we are not looking at these seven churches just from the historical stand point. We are not just reading their conditions almost two thousand years ago nor are we looking at them in a prophetic sense as if they represent the whole of church history. But we would like to see these seven churches together.

"He that hath an ear let him hear what the Spirit says to the church." Vocation follows vision. Vocation should be the practical expression of the vision seen. Vocation makes the vision practically seen by all. Vocation should correspond with vision, and probably that is the reason in the letters to the seven churches every letter begins with something of Christ as we have already seen in the first chapter. Whenever a vocation and a vision are separated, whenever there is a discrepancy between the vision and the vocation, you know there is failure. If there is contradiction between the vision and the vocation then the failure is great.

At the time of the apostle John when our Lord Jesus looked upon His church during that time, He found that there was much that did not correspond to Himself. The Lord had not yet removed any of these lampstands nor had the Lord spewed any of them out of His mouth. The Lord still recognized these churches as His, and they were still continuing outwardly as usual, and in each one of them there were commendable virtues. And yet when the Lord tried to measure Himself with the churches, He found there was much discrepancy and sometimes great contradictions. It is for this reason that the Lord Jesus is walking in the midst of the seven golden lampstands. He is there to reprove, to restore, to recover, and it is with this background that the call for the overcomer comes forth.

Dear brothers and sisters, if the Lord Jesus should walk among His churches today, do you think we are in a better position or in a worse position? Not to say that there is much lacking in the inward reality and even in the outward form. We wonder whether the Lord Jesus would even recognize us. And if this is the case then certainly the call to overcome is most urgent. In each of these seven letters there is the call to overcome. We are not able to go into details, but I think probably it will be of some help if we just pick out some of the important points and then try to find what constitutes that call. What is the call to overcome? Where forth should we overcome? In what place have we fallen? Who will be overcomers?

The Church in Ephesus

The first letter is to the church in Ephesus. Now if we know anything of the history of that church, as we read in the book of Acts, you know that the church in Ephesus had a very good beginning. The Word of God prospered in that city. Paul stayed there for years, and the Word of God prospered greatly, with many coming and confessing their sins. They burned all their books of magic which were many. In other words, there was first love in that church in Ephesus. They loved the Lord with a perfect heart, and that is the reason we have Paul's letter to the Ephesians. We know that this letter reveals to us the very height of spiritual knowledge and wisdom. It is the full knowledge of God.

Why is it that Paul was able to communicate the mystery of Christ, the mystery of God to that church which he could not do to the church at Corinth? The church at Corinth boasted of itself great knowledge. They thought that they had the knowledge, that they were not behind anybody in knowledge; but knowledge puffs up. And because they were full of this kind of knowledge Paul was not able to communicate to them the full counsel of God. But Paul was free to communicate to the Ephesians the mystery of Christ. Why? It is because they were a people of love. In the letter to the Ephesians the word love is mentioned (if I counted right) seventeen times—love, love, love. It is because they loved God, it opened the avenue to real knowledge. If you want to gather information, if you want to gather mental knowledge, so to speak, love is not required. You may accumulate great knowledge without love, but if you want to know God in the real way, love is the secret. It is not by pouring over books; it is by loving God. And the letter to the Ephesians concludes with a most wonderful verse. I do not know if you have noticed that in chapter 6:24, "Grace be with all them that love our Lord Jesus Christ with a love incorruptible."

In the letter to the Corinthians Paul concluded his letter by saying, "If anyone does not love the Lord

Jesus Christ, let him be anathema." But here he says, "May the grace be with all them who love our Lord Jesus Christ with an incorruptible love." This church, this people loved God with an incorruptible love, not with love that is corruptible which is human love. But they loved with a love incorruptible, the divine love. They were so filled with Christ and constrained by the love of Christ that they loved God with an incorruptible love. That is the church in Ephesus.

But when the apostle John was used of God to write the second letter to the Ephesians in the book of Revelation, there were many outward manifestations which were actually the result of their inward love towards God. These outward manifestations in the beginning were the consequence of their inward love of God, but after some years these outward manifestations continued. They looked very well, very commendable, and they continued on. Yet the inward flame was gone. The Lord Jesus said, "I am against you. In spite of all the good things you have, all these outward things you have, I am against you. The Lord is very hard: "I know all your good things, but I am against you." Oh, if we know the heart of God we can even sense the agony, agitation in the heart of God. I am against you because you have left your first love. Think! From whence have you fallen? Repent; otherwise I will remove the lampstand. In other words, there will be no testimony of Jesus.

I do not know whether you can find the reason why they left their first love. The Lord said, "You think; wherefore have you fallen?" There must be some reason for them to fall away from their first love, but I wonder if you can find the reason. The Scriptures seem to be silent on it. What is the reason wherefore they have fallen? On what point, for what reason, in what particular occasion marked the downfall, the decline of their love? I cannot find anything specific. If you can find it please let me know because there does not seem to be any specific reason. We can only take it in the more general principle, and remember, there is a principle.

In Proverbs 16:18 it says, "Pride goeth before destruction, and a haughty spirit before a fall." That is the general principle. "Pride goes before destruction and a haughty spirit before a fall." I wonder if the church in Ephesus fell on that point. Because of their love towards God, He had so privileged them with such a full knowledge of Him probably, gradually, they began to be proud of themselves. They had plenty of reason to be proud, but instead of looking off unto the Lord, they began to look into themselves: "How much we love, how much we love," and as they began to be proud of their spiritual achievement, of their spiritual condition, as some people put it, they began to have spiritual pride, and probably this is where they fell. They began to think of themselves instead of thinking of Him.

"Pride goes before destruction, and a haughty spirit before a fall." Maybe, I do not know, they fell for that particular reason.

Dear brothers and sisters, this is the danger that is ever present with those who are a little more privileged by God. If you are not so privileged you really have no reason to be proud, but if you are somewhat favored and privileged, the danger is that you begin to feel you have become somebody. Remember, that is where you begin to fall. You will fall from your first love. You may still maintain the outward form and continue on, and in a sense you will try your best to maintain it; that is pride. The inward flame is gone, but the outward form must continue because if it does not continue people will begin to know. But you are on an entirely false ground. That is the reason the Lord says, "If you do not repent, I will remove the testimony because it is not the testimony of Jesus anymore; it is the testimony of yourself that you are trying to maintain.

What is the call to overcome? The call to overcome is to be restored to the first love. That is absolute perfect first love towards Christ, towards God. Who is an overcomer? An overcomer is basically a lover. Do you think to be an overcomer you have to do some great things, accomplish some great tasks? No, to be an overcomer just requires one thing—to be a lover of God. That is all that is required. That is the call of an overcomer.

The Church in Smyrna

The second letter is to Smyrna. We know that this church suffered a great deal, so the call there is for faithfulness unto the end. As Christ emptied Himself and became a Man, as Christ humbled Himself as a Man and became obedient unto God even unto death and that the death of the cross, as Christ suffered to the very end, so the call to us is that we too may be faithful. Anyone who is faithful to God must suffer. These two things go together. We must suffer many persecutions in order to enter into the kingdom of God. If we follow the Lamb whithersoever He goes, we have to walk the way of the cross because this is the way. Are we willing to suffer for Him? for His sake? Are we ready to follow all the way with Him even if it means death? Sometimes we wonder why He does not deliver us. He ought to; if we are so faithful to Him He ought to deliver us. But here in the letter it says, "Some of you will be put into prison. Worse things will happen yet, as if God just stands back and allows everything to happen. Are you offended? Are you willing to follow Him fully, faithful even unto death?

What is the call of an overcomer? What is an overcomer? An overcomer is a martyr. It is one who bears the cross and follows the Lord. Very often I have this kind of feeling, Oh if God will give me the privilege of being a martyr. Whenever we read the stories of Christian martyrs, we are stirred in our very being. Oh, how we long that we may be privileged. But you are already privileged without knowing it, and you are always trying to get away from it. A living martyr suffers more than a dead martyr. But are we willing?

We live in a time as the apostle says, "People love themselves." We live in a time of self-love. We love ourselves too much, especially in this country. We will not allow ourselves to suffer even a little bit. We will go to the uttermost for ourselves. This is incompatible with the love of God. Are we willing to be a living martyr? Are we willing to follow the Lamb whithersoever He goes? Or do we just go to a certain limit and say, "Now so far and no more"? Just like in the Song of Solomon when the bride said: "Come back, I am not going with You, but You come back to me." However, you will find that He will never come back; He always goes on. Oh, if we want to go on with Him, we have to go on; He will not come back. An overcomer is a martyr, a lover.

The Church in Pergamum

The third letter is to Pergamum and there you find worldliness, the doctrine of Balaam, the mixing of the people of Israel with the Midianites. That is worldliness. When Satan failed in destroying the church by persecution, he tried to endorse it and give favors to the church. That is where worldliness comes in. On the one hand, the doctrine of Balaam is worldliness, on the other hand, the teaching of the Nicolaitans is professionalism. Here you find worldliness and professionalism come together. They always go together. Is it not that we are in a worse position than the church in Pergamum at that time? Oh, how the world has a great place in Christianity, and professionalism is prevailing everywhere. The call to overcome is the call to be separated. Come out of the world; come out of professionalism and be united with the real One. So an overcomer is basically a separatist.

The Church in Thyatira

The fourth letter is to the church at Thyatira. In that church there was not only corrupt conduct but there was corrupt teaching. The church was reduced into a corrupted system. It is like a mustard seed that has grown abnormally into a big tree, and all the birds of the air rest upon its branches. It has become a big system full of corruption, and yet it boasts of mystery and superstition. It is a gigantic system, and the call of the Lord is for purity. We are living in the time of great mixture, and what the Lord is looking for is pureness. "Blessed are the pure in heart for they shall see God" (Matthew 5:8). We do not know what that mystery is, the mystery of Satan, and do not try to know it. We are to know only what has been given to us, once delivered to the saints. People may call you ignorant, but blessed are the pure in heart for they shall see God. The call for overcomers is the call for purity. I believe that as the age is coming to a close God is looking more and more for purity, for pureness. When the thing is pure, it may be reduced to very little, but it is pure, and that is what God wants. The overcomers are the pure in heart; they know nothing but God.

The Church in Sardis

The fifth letter is to the church in Sardis. They have a name that is living, but they are dead. In other words, they have a form, but it is without life. What God is looking for today is life, not just a name. You may have had a good name in the past, you may have inherited a good name, but what God is looking for is life. Is there life there? Is there true life there? Why is it that the church in Sardis lost its life? In the very beginning of that letter the Lord said, "He is the one who has the seven spirits." When you get lost, when you lose your contact with the Holy Spirit, with the Spirit of God, you miss life. Life is Christ. Christ is life, but that life can only be experienced in the Holy Spirit. It is only when we are in living relationship, in living communication with the Spirit of God, that you are full of the life of Christ. Once that contact is lost life recedes. The name remains, but the life is finished. So it is most important for those who respond to God, to Christ, to maintain a continuous living relationship with the Holy Spirit. The anointing that is in you shall teach you in all things, and if you obey the anointing you shall abide in Him, abide in Christ. That is where you find life.

The Church in Philadelphia

The sixth letter is to the church in Philadelphia. What is it that the Lord is looking for in that church? I think probably what the Lord is looking for is this: "The Lord said, you have a little power." The Lord is looking for power, spiritual power in that church. You have a little power, but that little power is real power. Sometimes we may have a great deal of power, but it may not be real power. The Lord is looking for spiritual power. Where does that power come from? First, it comes from: "You have not denied My name." This means they have been continuously under the authority of the name of our Lord Jesus. "You have kept My word" which means the word of My patience, the word of the cross, and "you love one another" which is Philadelphia, brotherly love. On the basis of these three things you are under the authority of the Lord, of the heavens, you have walked the way of the cross, kept the word of my patience, and you have loved one another. This is power; this is spiritual power. It may not seem to be very great to the world, yet the Lord said, "You have a little power; that's it! That is the power I am looking for." Are we powerful before God? Do we have power before God?

The Church in Laodicea

The seventh letter is to the church in Laodicea. What the Lord is looking for in that church is reality. We know that the church in Laodicea lived in pretension, a falsehood. They said, "We are rich; we are not lacking anything. We have everything." Probably they did have something in the beginning, yet the Lord said, "You do not know that you are poor, miserable, naked." In other words, they were living in a falsehood; they were not living in reality. And the Lord suggested to them, advised them, to buy gold refined by fire, living faith, to buy white garments, the righteousness of the saints, practical righteousness, and eye salve, spiritual insight. They had to pay a cost to purchase these things, but the Lord really desires reality. He is the Amen, the reality, the true life.

Dear brothers and sisters, we are living in a world of falsehood. And very often even in our Christian world there is much that is false. We are deceiving ourselves; we are under a great deception, and we really need the Spirit of God to awaken us, to see how much is real and how much is unreal. One day that which is unreal must pass away, and when that day comes we will not know how poor we really are. Only that which remains counts; the other does not matter. So the Lord is looking for reality, spiritual reality. Now all these are real in Christ. He is the Son of man full of life. He is full of life, full of light, full of glory, full of righteousness, full of love, full of everything. This is what He is, and this is what He is looking for in His church, what He is looking for in you and in me. All the other does not really matter.

The Lord is Looking for Himself in His Church

Today the call is out: "He that has an ear let him hear what the Spirit says to the churches." The Spirit of God is speaking, but do we have the ear to hear? He is looking for Himself in His church. That is what He is looking for. You may have many things in your life that are good, but that is not what He is looking for in you. He is trying to find Himself in His church. Will the Lord find Himself in His church? How much can He find among His own? That which corresponds to Him, that which responds to Him, constitutes the nature of overcomers. So our Lord Jesus is *the* Overcomer, and He is calling us to overcome. An overcomer is not a superman, he is not a giant, he is not one who has done something great and spectacular. An overcomer is basically a lover, a martyr, a separated one, pure in heart, full of His life, spiritual power, and reality. In other words, he is one who responds to the Lord. Or we can use the word that is very popular now; he is a normal Christian, a normal Christian. So may the Lord be gracious to us.

Shall we pray:

Oh Lord, do open our eyes to see Thee as the Overcomer full of life, full of glory, that we may be so taken up with Thyself that our whole being, our whole attention may be focused upon Thee. We may forget all the other things, but seeking for one thing only that Thyself shall be formed in us. Oh, how we praise and thank Thee that Thou are not looking for any foreign things in our lives; Thou are just looking for Thyself in us. And we do desire to give ourselves to Thee that Thou may have a greater place in our lives, a greater and greater place that Thy heart may be satisfied. We ask in the precious name of our Lord Jesus. Amen.

3—The Making of Overcomers

May we look to the Lord in prayer:

Our heavenly Father, we do pray that the vision of Christ the Victor may ever be before us. When we are surrounded by things, by happenings that seem to be depressing, confusing and oppressing, we pray that in the very innermost of our hearts we can see Christ the Conqueror. Oh, how we praise and thank Thee that we can claim Him as our Overcomer. How we praise and thank Thee that by Him we too shall overcome. So we do pray that this vision may ever be before our eyes no matter what happens. We do commit this hour into Thy hand, and we claim Thy victory over this hour. We pray that the enemy may not in any way interfere with Thy work. We ask Thee that Thou will claim Thy victory over us, over the whole gathering for tonight. We commit this hour into Thy hand. Oh, how we desire to worship Thee because Thou art the changeless One. We ask in the precious name of our Lord Jesus. Amen.

We have been looking at two glorious scenes. First, we saw the glory of our Redeemer, the Lion of the tribe of Judah, the Lamb slain standing before the throne, Christ the Overcomer. Then we saw the vision of Christ as the Son of man walking in the midst of the seven golden candlesticks, looking for Himself in His own church, and for this reason the call to overcome has come to us. Now we would like to see another wonderful scene, and it is also in Revelation.

Revelation 7:9-17—After these things I saw, and lo, a great crowd, which no one could number, out of every nation and tribes and peoples and tongues, standing before the throne, and before the Lamb, clothed with white robes, and palm branches in their hands. And they cry with a loud voice, saying, Salvation to our God who sits upon the throne, and to the Lamb. And all the angels stood around the throne, and the elders, and the four living creatures, and fell before the throne upon their faces, and worshipped God, saying, Amen: Blessing, and glory, and wisdom, and thanksgiving, and honour, and power, and strength, to our God, to the ages of ages. Amen.

And one of the elders answered, saying to me, These who are clothed with white robes, who are they, and whence came they? And I said to him, My lord, thou knowest. And he said to me, These are they who come out of the great tribulation, and have washed their robes, and have made them white in the blood of the Lamb. Therefore are they before the throne of God, and serve him day and night in his temple, and he

3—The Making of Overcomers

that sits upon the throne shall spread his tabernacle over them. They shall not hunger any more, neither shall they thirst any more, nor shall the sun at all fall on them, nor any burning heat; because the Lamb which is in the midst of the throne shall shepherd them, and shall lead them to fountains of waters of life, and God shall wipe away every tear from their eyes.

The Jewish Remnant

In this 7th chapter of the book of Revelation, there is actually more than one scene. Before the portion which we have just read, there is the scene of the hundred and forty-four thousand of the tribes of Israel. After the Lamb has opened the sixth seal and before He opens the seventh seal, this 7th chapter is placed between these two seals. In the sixth seal that we find in the preceding chapter, the 17th verse: "because the great day of his wrath is come, and who is able to stand?" The great day of the wrath of God and of the Lamb is coming, and who is able to stand that day? But before the seventh seal is opened we find two wonderful scenes. On the one hand, out of the twelve tribes of Israel there are one hundred and forty-four thousand being sealed with the seal of God.

Now I will have to do a little interpretation. I hope you will not mind, but if you do not see eye to eye with me, I am quite willing to be corrected.

However, I do not intend to force you to see my way.
Again I will say that interpretation is interpretation;
it is not the Bible. We believe the Word of God even
though sometimes we may interpret it a little
differently. But what I would like to say is that the
interpretation is not important. What is important is
that we desire to see something that is very
significant on this matter of overcomers. Now if you
can get that, you can forget all the interpretations.
Thus I will try to interpret a little bit.

The four angels who hold the four winds of the
earth have to wait before they can blow upon the
earth. Symbolically, it means that before a greater
tribulation, a greater destruction can come upon the
earth, which is the great day of the wrath of God and
of the Lamb, God stays the hands of these angels. He
said, "Wait a minute; let me do something first."
Another angel ascending from the sun rising having
the seal of the living God, said, "Do not hurt the
earth and the seas until I have sealed the servants of
our God on their foreheads" (v. 3). So here you find
this angel is sealing the foreheads of the bondservants
of our God, and those who are sealed belong to the
twelve tribes of Israel. I personally believe this is
Israel. Out of the twelve tribes of Israel, before the
greater destruction comes upon the earth, God seals
one hundred and forty-four thousand, a round
number. Of course, the twelve tribes of Israel are
Israel as a nation, and there must be many more

people than a hundred and forty-four thousand. In other words, not every Israelite is sealed. Only a hundred and forty-four thousand out of the tribes of Israel are sealed with the seal of God.

I believe we know what sealing means. When God puts His seal, it means that God claims that which is sealed as His own; He claims His ownership. God acknowledges that this is Mine; it belongs to Me. And because it belongs to Him, therefore it is under His protection.

In the Old Testament in the book of Ezekiel, the 9th chapter, the prophet Ezekiel experienced something of this even during his time. He was taken by the Spirit of God into the temple in Jerusalem, and there he was shown all the abominations and abominable things that the people of God were doing in the temple. Then he saw six men with their destroying weapons. They came and stood by the altar, and then another man who was clothed in white linen with a writer's ink-horn by his side came too. And God said, "Before the six men with their destroying weapons went forth to destroy this man with the writer's ink-horn, he will first put a mark upon those who are moaning and groaning for the abominations in the city. He will put a mark, a Tau, like a cross upon the foreheads of those who moan, of those who groan with the groaning of God. And after the sealing was finished, the six men followed, starting from the temple." Judgment began at the house of God, and these six men would strike down, would smite everyone who did not have the seal upon their forehead, and the prophet Ezekiel was there. So this is the same picture in the Old Testament that we see in the book of Revelation.

Again, God is sealing His people. The twelve tribes of the nation normally belong to God; every Israelite belongs to God and is supposed to be God's bondservant. What else can they be? But in actuality when you come down to reality, out of the twelve tribes of Israel only one hundred and forty-four thousand are sealed. In other words, God acknowledged them as His. The Lord knows those who are His, and they are sealed. Usually, we say this is a Jewish remnant at the end of this age. When the end of this age is approaching, there will be a Jewish remnant. We call it a remnant because it is just a very small part of the whole nation, yet this remnant is faithful unto God. God owns them as His, and He protects them from hurt and harm. Now this is the first scene that we have seen, and parallel with this scene, we have before us what we shall consider for this time.

The Church of God

The apostle John said, "After these things I saw and behold a great multitude which no man could number out of every nation and tribes and people and tongues." Whenever you come to such a description in the Scripture: "Out of every nation and tribe and people and tongue," immediately you know that it refers to the church of God. The church of God is composed of those whom God has chosen out of every nation and tribe and people and tongue and gathered them unto one name, the name of our Lord Jesus. That is the church. I will put it in a term our brother has used, this is the new Israel. We find in the first part the old Israel, Israel according to the flesh, and here in the second part is the new Israel, the church of God. But when you read further, there are more descriptions which do not seem to fit in with the church in general. They are standing before the throne and before the Lamb. Now this is the part of interpretation.

We read of this great crowd which is numberless. I do thank God for this numberless crowd who are standing before the throne and before the Lamb. According to the order of the book of Revelation and the time factor of the book of Revelation, this scene is between the sixth and seventh seal. This is seen before the blowing of the seven trumpets, not to say the blowing of the last trumpet. We know from I Thessalonians chapter 4 that the Lord shall descend from heaven, and there will be the voice of the archangel, the sounding of the trumpet, and the shout. Those who are dead in Christ shall be raised from the dead, and those who remain alive shall be transformed, and we shall all be taken up to the clouds to meet the Lord in the air.

In I Corinthians 15, when the last trumpet is sounded, the dead shall be raised, and those who live shall be transformed. So when you put these two together, you will find that the day will come when the last trumpet shall be sounded. All those who have died in Christ throughout the centuries shall be raised from the dead, and those who remain alive shall be transformed, and we shall all be caught up to the air to meet our Lord who has descended from heaven.

The Throne

However, the seven seals have not been opened yet. None of the trumpets have been sounded; certainly the last trumpet has not been sounded. And these men are not standing in the clouds nor in the air, but they are standing before the throne and before the Lamb. Where is the throne and where is the Lamb at that time?

In Revelation 4 it says, "I saw the heaven opened, and I was taken up in the Spirit and saw a throne. The throne is in heaven. Then in chapter 5, where is the Lamb? "The Lamb slain standing before the throne." In other words, it is in heaven, not in the clouds nor in the air; it is way up in heaven. And these men are already standing before the throne and before the Lamb, even before He descends to the clouds, to the air. I feel this is almost like what we read in Luke 21:36: "Watch therefore, praying at every season, that ye may be accounted worthy to escape all these things which are about to come to pass, and to stand before the Son of man."

In Revelation 12:5 it says, "And she brought forth a male son, who shall shepherd all the nations with an iron rod; and her child was caught up to God and to his throne." Here is a countless crowd who are standing before the throne as if they are there to welcome the Lord back to this earth.

Clothed in White Robes

Secondly, they are clothed in white robes. In Revelation 3:4-5a, in the letter to the church in Sardis the Lord says, "But thou hast a few names in Sardis which have not defiled their garments, and they shall walk with me in white, because they are worthy. He that overcomes, he shall be clothed in white garments."

This is a promise to the overcomers in the church at Sardis that they would be clothed with white garments. These garments are made white because they have been washed in the blood of the Lamb. When we come to God, He puts a robe over us. We can use that parable of the prodigal son: when the son comes back home, he is in rags, and the father says, "Take away the rags and put the best robe on him." In other words, we are clothed with Christ.

As we come to God we are clothed with Christ. Christ is our righteousness, and this is the best robe.

May I ask a question? Does that white robe need to be washed? Can that robe be defiled? We are clothed with Christ; Christ our righteousness. Can that righteousness be defiled? Does that righteousness need to be washed? Certainly not! Jesus Christ is the same yesterday, today and forever. He is righteous forever. He does not need to be washed; He never changes. The robe that we are clothed with by God, Christ our righteousness, does not need to be washed. It is forever white, pure and shiny, but the Bible tells us that we believers are clothed with two garments instead of one. We are clothed with Christ, yet there is another robe that we need to be clothed with.

The Embroidered Garment

Psalm 45 is a psalm which speaks of the king. It begins: "My heart is welling forth with a good matter: I say what I have composed touching the king." When we speak of the King, Christ our King, it is the pen of a ready writer. Oh, how his heart swells as he writes of the king! How glorious, how righteous, how majestic, how gracious; but as he is writing concerning the king, naturally he turns to the queen. In v. 13: "All glorious is the king's daughter within; her clothing is of wrought gold." The queen is clothed with a dress of wrought gold, a golden garment. Symbolically, gold speaks of God, the nature of God. It never changes. In other words, this woman is clothed with Christ our righteousness.

Verse 14: "She shall be brought unto the king in raiment of embroidery." Upon this dress of wrought gold she is also dressed with a dress of embroidered work. That is another garment, the second garment. The first garment speaks of Christ our righteousness, but this second garment is of embroidered work. The sisters know that when you are making a dress of embroidered work, you have to have patience, one stitch after another. It is done with great patience and according to a pattern, but after it is done it is most beautiful. After we are clothed with Christ then the Holy Spirit will begin to use His needle. He begins to work one stitch after another incorporating Christ into our very life. That is a very patient work, but the Holy Spirit is most patient. He is working one stitch after another according to Christ that we may not only be clothed with Christ but that He may be incorporated into our very being. It is an embroidered work.

Revelation 19 says, "This is the righteousnesses of the saints" (v. 8). Not only is Christ our righteousness, but Christ is so inwrought, so incorporated into us that it comes out as if it is our righteousness—the righteousnesses of the saints, and this is the second garment. I personally believe that this is what is meant here. It is not the first robe because it can never be defiled, but the second robe, so far as our practical life is concerned, so far as our standing before God is concerned, it can be defiled. Christ is our righteousness; it never changes. However, when it comes down to our daily life, our daily conduct, our daily conversation, our daily behavior it is the will of God that by the patient working of the Holy Spirit and the washing of the blood there might come forth a beautiful embroidered robe, but we have to say that very often we defile that robe. Very often we do not listen to the voice of the Spirit of God, and we allow our garment to be defiled by the world, and because of that it needs to be washed. "If we walk in the light as He is in the light we have fellowship one with another, and the blood of Jesus Christ God's Son cleanses us from all our unrighteousness" (I John 1:7). If we walk in the light the blood cleanses; this is how this white garment is washed in the blood.

Thirdly, they have palms in their hands. I think we all know that palms always stand for victory. When the Lord Jesus entered into Jerusalem for the last time you will remember that the people took branches of palms and went forth to meet Him, and they cried, "Hosanna, blessed is He who comes in the name of the Lord, the King of Israel" (John 12:13). Palms stand for victory. They waved the palms which means they are in the victory of Christ. We also know that in the house of God which Solomon built there were palm trees, cherubim and half-opened flowers all around the walls. The cherubim speak of the holiness of God. The cry of the cherubim is "Holy, holy, holy, Lord God Almighty." The palm tree speaks of victory, and the half-opened flowers speak of glory, the glory of life. Why is it half-opened? It is because it is still open.

From these descriptions we can see the parallel between the first part of chapter 7 and the second part of chapter 7, and it is logical to conclude that the one hundred and forty-four thousand sealed among the twelve tribes of Israel represent the Jewish remnant. Then this countless crowd standing before the throne and before the Lamb represent the overcomers of the church. That is why I feel most thankful to God. We often think of overcomers in terms of one or two, and it is true that in comparison with the church at large, in comparison with God's people, the overcomers may be just a minority. However, do not limit God because here you find a countless crowd; God has His countless overcomers. You may think you are the only overcomer, as the prophet Elijah thought, but God said, "I have seven thousand." Countless number! Thank God for that! I wonder if this countless crowd represents those overcomers in the seven churches in Asia; certainly they do. I wonder if this group represents all the overcomers in the church from the first century down through the ages. I believe it does.

Here you find this great crowd of overcomers standing before the throne and before the Lamb. It is a glorious scene. And they lead the song; they cry salvation unto our God who sits on the throne and unto the Lamb. They lead the singing. And their song is taken up and followed by the angels, and there is a great worship in heaven. It is a beautiful scene.

Then one of the elders asked the apostle John: "Do you know who they are? And where do they come from?" John said, "You know." I think John is very wise. Very often we are like Peter. We do not know what to say, but we have to say something, and in doing that we always say the wrong thing. I think John is very wise because he said, "You know." Oh, how we like to guess. But John said, "You tell me who they are, where do they come from?" And this is the point that we want to fellowship on.

Ones Who Come Out of the Great Tribulation

And he said to me, "These are they who come out of the great tribulation, and have washed their robes, and have made them white in the blood of the Lamb (v. 14). They come out of great tribulation. Forgive me now for my little interpretation. Personally, I do not think this points to the great tribulation of three and a half years which will come at the end of this age. Personally, I believe this great tribulation is a general term. Where do these overcomers come from? They come out of great tribulation. When we think of overcomers, we are always thinking in terms of victory, triumph, superiority, high up, ascendency. That is true; the outcome is ascendency, but do you know that to reach this ascendency you have to go through deep waters? It is easy to pray: "Oh Lord, make me an overcomer." But if the Lord tries to make you an overcomer, you will cry out and say, "Stop Your hand." How are these overcomers made? Where do they come from? They come out of great tribulation. Oh, look at our Lord Jesus, *the* Overcomer. Did God prepare an easy, smooth and prosperous way for our Lord while He was on earth? Quite the contrary. We find that because our Lord so pleased the Father, therefore He was beset with tribulation. He was oppressed, afflicted, a Man of sorrows, acquainted with grief. He was as a lamb sheared of its wool, of all its beauty and glory. He was to be crucified on that cross of shame and curse. That is where He came from.

When you read the lives of the apostles, you find the same thing. A dear sister in the Lord, Miss Annie Johnson Flint, once wrote a poem. I believe if you do not know her you must know her poem:

> God hath not promised skies always blue,
> Flower strewn pathways all our lives through;
> God hath not promised sun without rain,
> Joy without sorrows, peace without pain.

But God hath promised strength for the day,
Rest for the labor, light for the way.
Grace for the trials, help from above,
Unfailing sympathy, undying love."

Our concept of Christian life is the concept of smooth sailing all the way. But this is not the way overcomers are made. To overcome presupposes there are troubles, there are difficulties, there are problems, there are tribulations, there are oppressions, and there are pressures. To overcome means striving, pressing on, wrestling to the very end. It is not a picture of one who is sitting in a sedan chair and carried to heaven. It is a picture of one who is fighting his way through, dropping his blood all along the way. That is an overcomer.

I am very touched by what Paul says to the saints at Corinth in I Corinthians 4: "Already ye are filled; already ye have been enriched; ye have reigned without us; and I would that ye reigned, that we also might reign with you. For I think that God has set us the apostles for the last, as appointed to death. For we have become a spectacle to the world, both to angels and men. *We* are fools for Christ's sake, but *ye* prudent in Christ: *we* weak, but *ye* strong: *ye* glorious, but *we* in dishounor. To the present hour we both hunger and thirst, and are in nakedness, and buffeted, and wander without a home, and labour, working with our own hands. Railed at, we bless; persecuted, we suffer it; insulted, we entreat: we are become as the offscouring of the world, the refuse of all, until now" (vv. 8-13).

Two Types of Christians

The Corinthian Type

There are two types of Christians, the Corinthian type and the apostolic type. These Corinthian believers were already filled. They may not be emptied, but they were already filled. They had already become rich; they did not need to be poor in order to be rich like our Lord. They had already come to reign; they get to the throne without the cross. They were wise, very wise. They were very strong. I suppose if you do not know God, if you do not know God's way, you will say this is for me. Certainly to be a Christian is to be strong, to be a Christian is to be wise, to be a Christian is to be filled, to be a Christian is to become rich, to be a Christian is to reign. Now this is for me. Well, if you want to be the Corinthian type of Christian, you may have it.

The Apostolic Type

But the apostle said, "Not so with the apostles. They must be emptied in order to be filled. They must be poor in order to become rich, they must endure with Christ in order to reign with Him. They are as men doomed to death." And this is not just an exaggerated description; this is a fact. Men doomed to death, a spectacle unto the world, weak, poor for Christ, even unto the present hour. The situation does not improve—even unto the present hour. We will say it is all right to be hungry in the beginning, but Paul said even unto the present hour we are still in hunger and thirst. We are naked, buffeted, with no certain dwelling place, wanderers, reviled, we bless; persecuted, we endure; defamed, we entreat. We are made the filth of the world, the offscouring of the world, even unto now.

Do you want to be an overcomer? It is costly. Are you willing to be emptied? Are you willing to be reduced to poverty? Are you willing to be a fool for Christ? Are you willing to be a weak vessel? Are you willing to be the offscouring of all things? the filth of the world? Are you willing?

When our Lord Jesus called for His disciples, He said, "Unless a man denies himself, takes up his cross and follows me, he cannot be my disciple." You may substitute the word disciple for another word, overcomer. The Lord is calling for overcomers, but how is an overcomer made? "Deny yourself, take up your cross and follow me. He that loves his life shall lose it, but he who loses his life for my sake shall gain it to eternity" (see Matthew 10:37, Luke 9:23-24, Mark 8:34). This is what is meant by these men coming out of great tribulation. Are you waiting for the great tribulation to come? Your tribulation is great enough, and this means not only the things around us. It is true that if we love the Lord and press on, there will be tribulation coming upon us, no doubt about that, but this great tribulation includes much more. There will be trials, testings, and pressures.

Paul says in II Corinthians, "I have the sentence of death upon me, and I am pressed beyond my measure," but it is out of this experience that he knows the God who delivers. Paul's experience was in knowing that the grace of the Lord is sufficient, and he said, "When I am weak, then I am strong."

The Embroidered Work of the Holy Spirit

Who are the overcomers? They come out of great tribulation. Oh, as you follow the Lord you will meet crisis after crisis. There will be tribulations on all sides, and when you enter into these things, in a sense, it will reveal where you are standing and what you are. We do not know ourselves until we are put under pressure. Then we know what is in us. In the tribulation we realize our weaknesses. How we need the blood of the Lamb to cleanse us! Under tribulation sometimes we are so overwhelmed, and we need to repent and ask for the cleansing of the precious blood. If there is anyone who thinks that he does not need the blood of the Lamb because he is so strong that he never fails, beware lest you fall. All those who know God, all those who live very close to

God, if you read their biographies, you will find one thing invariably: the closer they draw near to God in their life experiences, the more they feel the need of the precious blood of the Lamb. Their garments are made white by the blood of the Lamb. This is the righteousnesses of the saints. Without tribulations we will not realize the need of the blood, but with tribulations we know how much we need the blood of the Lamb.

Dear brothers and sisters, as we follow the Lord, His way is the way of the cross. Not only the passions and the lust of our flesh need to be purified, but our whole soul needs to be purified. Our emotional life needs to be washed with the blood. It is only when we are faced with a crisis do we realize how impure our emotional life is. That is the reason why the Lord said, "If anyone loves their father and mother, and so on, more than me, he cannot be my disciple." He even put it in stronger terms: "If anyone does not hate his father and mother, and wife, and children, and brothers, and sisters, yea, and his own life, he cannot be my disciples (see Luke 14:26). In other words, our emotional life needs to be washed in the blood. You do not realize how impure your love is. You think you love the Lord like Peter, "Even if I go and have to die with You, I am quite ready. All the others may fall away but I will not." And sometimes we hope they do fall away so that we may prove our point. But Peter failed! Oh, it is only when there is a conflict, when there is a crisis, when there is a contradiction, a contrast, a cross, a tribulation that we see how much we need the cleansing of the blood. Oh, a sword enters into our soul, it divides and makes clear, and washes us clean. It creates that white garment made white by the blood.

Not only does our emotional life need to be purified, but our thought life, our mental life needs to be cleansed. You remember that occasion when the Lord Jesus began to reveal to Peter and the other disciples that He must go to Jerusalem, and there He would be rejected and die, but He would be raised up on the third day. Peter laid hold of the Lord and said, "Not so, Lord, be kind to yourself!" And the Lord turned around to Peter and said, "Satan, get thee behind me because you are not minding the mind of God; you are minding the flesh." How often we find our thought life needs to be washed, needs to be purified!

Of course, our volitional life, our will also needs to be purified. But is that all? No. In II Corinthians 7:1 it says, "Even our spirit needs to be purified." Not only does our flesh need to be purified, our spirit needs to be purified. It needs to be purified of that haughty spirit before a fall. It needs to be purified from a different spirit. The Lord said to John and James, "You do not know what kind of spirit you have. You do not have the spirit of the Lamb because you want fire to come down and burn that village in

Samaria" (see Luke 9:54). It is only when we enter into a trial, tribulation, pressure, and all these things that we begin to realize how much we need the blood of the Lamb.

That is how this embroidered work of the Holy Spirit is made. It is through the daily patient working of the Holy Spirit in our lives as we are faced with things, events, and crisis together with the washing of the blood. That makes up this beautiful white garment out of great tribulation. So we should not expect to be overcomers without paying the price of following the Lamb whithersoever He goes.

They Stand Before the Throne

But thank God, we read: "Therefore are they before the throne of God, and serve Him day and night in his temple, and he that sits upon the throne shall spread his tabernacle over them. They shall not hunger any more, neither shall they thirst any more, nor shall the sun at all fall on them, nor any burning heat; because the Lamb which is in the midst of the throne shall shepherd them, and shall lead them to fountains of waters of life, and God shall wipe away every tear from their eyes" (Revelation 7:15-17).

They shall stand before the throne of God because they are clothed with these two garments— the garment of gold and the garment of embroidered work. They are ready to stand before God. They shall serve Him day and night in the temple. It reminds me of Ezekiel 44: "God spoke to the sons of Zadok and said, "At the time when the people of Israel fell away from God, and the Levites went far away from God, but they kept the charge, and because of that they were able to minister unto the Lord; not minister unto the house but minister unto the Lord.""

They served God day and night in the temple because they had been faithful in the days of tribulation and trouble, and He that sits on the throne shall spread His tabernacle over them. He will shelter them. They have been wandering and now they have come home. They shall hunger no more nor thirst anymore. They have been hungering, they have suffered first, but no more and God shall wipe away every tear. Oh, this is the day of humiliation, not the day of glory. Glory is before us, but we have to follow the Lamb in humility, and this is how overcomers are made.

Let us pray:

> Our heavenly Father, we do praise and worship Thee that it is not just a limited number but a countless crowd that stands before the throne and before the Lamb. Oh, how we praise and thank Thee that the wife of the Lamb has made herself ready and she is given a robe of linen, white, pure and shiny. We have to acknowledge that it is all of grace. If there is anything that we can lay down it is the result of

Thy grace. Lord, we do pray that we may be those who on earth will follow the Lamb whithersoever He goes. If it means the way of the cross, let it be so. We praise and worship Thee because out of great tribulation the raiment shall be washed white. Oh Lord, do speak to us, do show us how overcomers are made. We ask in the precious name of our Lord Jesus. Amen.

4—The Task of Overcomers

May we look to the Lord in prayer:

Oh Lord, as we wait together before Thee, our prayer is that Thou will speak a word to each one of us. We know and we believe that Thy Word is life and Spirit to us, and how we long for Thy Word. We ask Thee that Thou will open our inner ear to hear, open our inner eye to see and open our heart to receive Thee into us. Oh Lord, we do commit this time into Thy hand. What has Thou to say to us? Thy servants are hearing. We do desire to come to Thy presence with a worshipping spirit because Thou are our God and our Lord, mighty to save, and worthy to be praised. We ask in Thy precious name. Amen.

I want to say at the very beginning that our brother Mr. Sparks has taken my message away this morning, but he has not taken my Lord away, and thank God he gives more of my Lord to me. The sustenance of our message this evening is almost the same as you have heard this morning, so I think probably I have more liberty to do a little interpretation.

Revelation 12:1-12—And a great sign was seen in the heaven: a woman clothed with the sun, and the moon under her feet, and upon her head a crown of twelve stars; and being with child she cried, being in travail, and in pain to bring forth.

And another sign was seen in the heaven: and behold, a great red dragon, having seven heads and ten horns, and on his heads seven diadems; and his tail draws the third part of the stars of the heaven; and he cast them to the earth. And the dragon stood before the woman who was about to bring forth, in order that when she brought forth he might devour her child. And she brought forth a male son, who shall shepherd all the nations with an iron rod; and her child was caught up to God and to his throne. And the woman fled into the wilderness, where she has there a place prepared of God, that they should nourish her there a thousand two hundred and sixty days.

And there was war in the heaven: Michael and his angels went to war with the dragon. And the dragon fought, and his angels; and he prevailed not, nor was their place found any more in the heaven. And the great dragon was cast out, the ancient serpent, he who is called Devil and Satan, he who deceives the whole habitable world, he was cast out into the earth, and his angels were cast out with him.

And I heard a great voice in the heaven saying, Now is come the salvation and the power and the kingdom of our God, and the authority of his Christ; for the accuser of our brethren has been cast out, who accused them before our God day and night: and they have overcome him by reason of the blood of the Lamb, and by reason of the word of their testimony, and have not loved their life even unto death. Therefore be full of delight, ye heavens, and ye that dwell in them. Woe to the earth and to the sea, because the devil has come down to you, having great rage, knowing he has a short time.

The Age before the Great Tribulation

In this chapter we find mentioned a thousand two hundred and sixty days. Later on, it is said that it is a time and times and half a time. In other words, what you have before you is three and a half years or forty-two months. Now if this means anything to us, I think immediately we can conclude that this scene concerns the end of this age. In other words, it is a scene of the end time. It is a scene that is seen immediately before the tribulation the great, three and a half years. Why do we call this three and a half years the tribulation the great? Because at that time the trinity of evil is upon the earth. Chapter 12 tells us that the red dragon, who is Satan, is cast out of the sky into the earth; Satan is upon the earth. In chapter 13 the first beast comes out of the sea, who is the antichrist, and out from the land comes the second beast, the false prophet. The trinity of evil is upon the earth, and what can you expect but the tribulation the great? If this interpretation is correct then we are dealing with the situation in the end times at the very end of this age just before the tribulation the great.

The Woman in Travail

What you see here first of all is a woman in travail. This woman is clothed with the sun and the moon under her feet. Upon her head is a crown of twelve stars, and she is in travail waiting to give birth to a child. Since our attention for these times is upon the overcomers, I do not think we should spend time in describing this woman. But if you have time you can read our dear brother Watchman Nee's book called "The Glorious Church" in which he tries to give us an interpretation of what this woman is. So I will just take from his book and say that this woman is the church at the end time, and she is in pain and travail. Of course, this immediately brings us back to Romans 8:22-23: "For we know that the whole creation groans together and travails in pain together until now. And not only that, but even we ourselves, who have the first-fruits of the Spirit, we also ourselves groan in ourselves, awaiting adoption," that is for sonship.

The Whole Creation is in Travail

The whole creation is under a heavy burden; it is subjected through vanity, not of its own will but because of Him who makes it so. After the fall of man the whole creation entered into vanity and the bondage of corruption. Ever since that time the whole creation is groaning and moaning instinctively. Even though the psalmist says, "The heavens declare the glory of God and the firmament shows His handiwork," which is true, yet on the other hand all the created things in this universe, in a sense, misrepresent God. Why? Because we find vanity and corruption everywhere. When you look at a beautiful flower as it begins to bud, then to open up, but at the height of its glory it fades away; it is corruption. It is the same with the trees as they grow and begin to spread out and are filled with leaves. They are beautiful, magnificent, but then the leaves begin to fall and then the tree is barren. There is nothing in this created world that is not under the bondage of corruption. Even the hills and the mountains have been there for centuries, yet if we had a spiritual ear to hear we could hear them crying out: "Why are we standing here year after year, century after century. What is the meaning of our existence?" The whole creation is groaning and waiting for something—for the liberty of the sons of God. How much more are we groaning who have the first fruits of the Spirit?

There is a groaning within God's people; there is a groaning in the church, and this groaning is a travail. It is an expectation for something, and the Bible says, "It is waiting for adoption." In other words, it is waiting for the placing of sons. We have the first fruits of the Spirit within us; we have the life of Christ within us, and now this life within us groans for growth, for maturity, for sonship.

Anyone who has the first fruits of the Spirit within him, anyone who has life in him cannot but feel the growing pains of life. There is within us a groaning, a desire to grow into full maturity, to grow into sonship. We are not content just to be little children playing around. There is a groaning within us to grow into responsibility, to grow into sympathy with God, and to grow into the concern and interest of God. This is the groaning within us. The Spirit is groaning within us for growth, and without us all the things on this earth are pressing upon us and making us groan.

Sometimes when we think of the problems of this world—the wars, pestilences, earthquakes, famines, problems, all these things on the earth—we wonder why. Why does God allow these things to happen on the earth? Certainly He is not interested in wars or pestilences, certainly it is not the will of God to make the people of this world suffer so much. Then why is it that we have all these things going on around us? The whole earth is under a heavy burden and pressure. The whole earth is under tribulation, pain and suffering, almost to the point of being unbearable. It cannot bear anymore. If we look at these things by themselves, probably some may feel that even their very faith is being shaken.

When our Lord Jesus spoke on the Mount of Olives in Matthew 24 concerning the things that are coming, He said, "There will be wars and rumors of war, there will be pestilences, there will be famine, there will be false prophets, and all these things coming upon the earth; these are the beginning of throes, the beginning of birth pangs." The whole world is in travail, especially the church of God which has been and is in travail. When a woman is in travail, it is true that it is very painful. She is going through the process of death, and it is something to be afraid of. She trembles under the pressure, yet on the other hand, such suffering is not negative, it is not in vain because it is birth pangs. After the pangs there will be joy unspeakable, joy because a child is born. All the things that are happening in the world today—pathetic things, tragic things, terrible, frightening, and shattering things, but if you see God's purpose you know that these are but birth pangs. Yes, they are painful, but these will bring forth something very positive for God.

After the Lord has ascended and the world begins to go through the throes, the birth pangs, how much more the travail and the birth pangs will be increased in intensity and in recurrence for us who are living near the end time because something or someone is going to come forth. The woman is in travail to give birth to a child. The whole church of God today has been under persecution, trials and tribulations through these twenty centuries, and when it comes down to our time which is approaching the end days, we find that the church is under intense suffering. Oh, if we only see the church of God throughout the world, we may think we can sit here very peacefully without any interruption because we can talk of the Lord, we can fellowship with one another without any fear. However, at this very hour there are many places on the earth where God's people cannot meet together. Even when two or three try to gather for a little time, they are in fear and trembling less they be found. We do not know the sufferings of God's people. We do not know what they have gone through and are going through. The little that we have heard make us tremble. We wonder how it can be that God allows such sufferings, such persecutions, such travailing to His own people, but it happens. And it has increased in intensity, in numbers, in recurrence because the church is to give birth to a child.

The Red Dragon

When this woman is in travail, there is another scene in heaven. There is the great red dragon with seven heads, ten horns, and upon its head there are seven diadems. His tail draws a third part of the stars from heaven and casts them upon the earth. The dragon is standing before the woman who is about to deliver so that he may devour her child when he comes forth.

This great dragon is red, and red is the color of blood; he is blood thirsty. Our Lord Jesus said in the gospel of John chapter 8 that this red dragon was a murderer from the very beginning. He has not told the truth because there is no truth in him; this is the adversary of God and of man. Further on, there is a full description given of this dragon. He is not only called the red dragon, he is the old serpent. Of course, immediately, we remember the scene in the garden of Eden. That serpent with his craftiness deceived Eve into taking the fruit of the tree of the knowledge of good and evil in rebellion against God. The old serpent is called the devil and Satan. He is the evil spirit, the adversary of God and of man, the deceiver of the whole world. Oh, how he deceives! And lastly, he is the accuser. Not only does Satan accuse us before God, but he accuses us in our conscience to make us so troubled that we dare not approach the throne of grace. And here is Satan and his kingdom with all his power standing before the woman waiting to devour the child that is to come forth.

The Child

The focal point here is the child. The woman here is going to give birth, and the dragon is standing before the woman waiting to jump, not upon the woman, but upon the child that is to be brought forth. Satan is fully aware of the significance of this child that is to be born. So the conflict here is over the child, the male child.

Who is this male child? Who is this one that is so important in the eyes of Satan? Who is he that the woman is about to bring forth? In other words, the travail of the woman is centered upon one thing. The meaning of her travail is in that child that is to come forth. This is the meaning of the woman. On the other hand, the meaning of the menace, the opposition, the assault of the enemy is also the child. The child has become a marked person, *a marked person*. Now who is he? If the woman is the church at the end time, then this child cannot be the church too. The child is in the womb of the woman, and the child comes out of the woman. Now who is this child?

We find there is a description of this child. "And she was delivered of a son, a man child who is to rule all the nations with a rod of iron" (Revelation 12:5). That is the description. This child is destined to rule all the nations with an iron rod. Who is he? The same clause appears in the book of Revelation three times.

In Revelation 2:26-27: "And he that overcomes, and he that keeps unto the end my works, to him will I give authority over the nations, and he shall shepherd them with an iron rod; as vessels of pottery are they broken in pieces, as I also have received from my Father." This is a promise to the overcomers in the church in Thyatira who are to be given authority over all the nations, and they shall rule the nations with an iron rod. That is the second place or according to order, the first place.

The third time is in Revelation 19:15: "And out of his mouth goes a sharp two-edged sword, that with it he might smite the nations; and he shall shepherd them with an iron rod."

We know this is a description of the Lord, the Overcomer, our Lord Jesus. He shall come upon the earth with a sword out of His mouth and smite the enemies, and He shall rule all the nations with an iron rod. This is our Lord Jesus Christ.

The Overcomers of the Church

So this description in Revelation 2 is used for the overcomers of the church, and in Revelation 19 it is used for our Lord the Overcomer. Now in Revelation 12:5, who does it refer too? Does it mean our Lord or does it mean the overcomers of the church? In the first place, the woman comes out of the man. You remember that God put Adam to sleep and out of his side He took a rib and built a woman with it. The woman comes out of the man, and of course the child comes out of the woman. So in the first place, we cannot say that Christ comes out of the church; the church comes out of Christ. Out of the side of Christ, out of the heart of Christ, out of the love of Christ, out of His blood and life that were given, the church is born and is built. This woman cannot mean Mary, the mother of Jesus, even though Mary is a most honored woman. We honor her very much, but we cannot say she is clothed with the sun, and the moon is under her feet, and she wears a crown of twelve stars. This is not her description. So if the woman is the church then the male child cannot be Christ personally.

Secondly, this scene of birth happened just before the great tribulation, the thousand, two hundred and sixty days. Immediately, after his birth, the three and a half years of the tribulation the great, are ushered in. Now this does not happen in the life of Christ. After He was born, He lived on this earth thirty-three and a half years, and it is only after He has left that the prophecy in Matthew 24 begins to be unfolded. So we cannot say this refers to Christ.

Thirdly, after Christ is born He is not immediately caught up to God and to the throne. If that were the case there would be no salvation to us. After He was born He remained on this earth for thirty-three and a half years to accomplish the work of redemption. It is only after the redemption work was finished that He was caught up to heaven. But the moment this male child is born he is caught up to heaven.

Fourthly, this male child is a corporate person, "For the accuser of our brethren has been cast out, who accused them before our God day and night, and they have overcome him by reason of the blood of the Lamb, and by reason of the word of their testimony, and have not loved their life even unto death. Therefore be full of delight, ye heavens, and ye that dwell in them" (12:10b-11). Everything is plural. This plural child is a corporate child, not a personal Christ, but a corporate child. Again I will say this is interpretation and not the substance. If we allow these to be some basis of interpretation, then we can almost say that if the woman represents the church at the end time, then this child is the overcomers at the end time.

In chapters 2 and 3 the overcomers of the church are in the first century because these seven churches existed in the first century. Even though the church was in declension, yet out of this general condition came forth overcomers. So these are overcomers of the first century.

In chapter 7 we find a countless crowd standing before the throne and before the Lamb. These are the overcomers throughout the twenty centuries. In each century there are overcomers. Thank God for that! God has never left Himself without His witnesses on this earth. No matter how the church has fallen, no matter how she has deviated from the original purpose of God, He has His own to maintain the testimony of Jesus throughout the twenty centuries. We find that in chapter 7.

In chapter 12 you find the overcomers at the end time just before the return of the Lord. This child is in the womb of the woman. In other words, the overcomers are in the church. The travail of the woman is for the travail of the child. Or we may put it in another way: the woman is in travail in order that a child may be born, and then she is satisfied. The essence of the church is in the child, the overcomers. What the church ought to be is expressed, is substantiated, is precipitated, is brought into being in that male child. The overcomers are not those who are in a sense entirely separated from the church. Rather, the overcomers of the church represent what the church ought to be before God, and because of that the controversy is not over the woman at that time but over the male child. Satan knows better than we do. He knows that he does not need to be bothered with the woman too much. His first interest is in the child because he knows that the child is the instrument in God's hand to defeat him and his kingdom. We call this male child the overcomers at the end time. What have they done?

From a human standpoint the child has done nothing. The woman is in travail, but the child has not done anything. However, the strange thing is that when he is born, he has overcome the adversary of God and of man.

Our thought of overcomers is usually wrapped up with the great work we have done, the earth-seeking work we have done, the spectacular things we have accomplished. Everybody can see that we have done a great thing. But when we look at the child from the outward standpoint, he has done nothing. Not only has the child done nothing, he is also unseen. That which is seen is minor, that which is unseen is the essential. We like to see; we are attracted by things that can be seen. Why? Because these things nourish our flesh. We thrive on such food, but when God is doing His work, it may not be seen by anyone. It is not something to be seen, but it is something that will affect the unseen world. The child has done nothing. We do not see him do anything, yet the Bible says they overcome Satan.

They Overcome by the Blood

They overcome by reason of the blood of the Lamb. They overcome not because they have their own merits to boast of; they have none. They overcome because out of great tribulation they learn the preciousness of the blood of the Lamb. They have their garments washed white in the blood of the

Lamb. They are not supermen; they are not infallible. They have fallen, they have much weakness, yet they know the value of the blood of the Lamb. By the blood they have boldness to enter into the throne of grace, and by the blood they can stand before the adversary and say, "Get away." Their boldness is based upon the blood of the Lamb, not upon themselves.

They Overcome by Their Testimony

Secondly, "they overcome by reason of the word of their testimony." What is their testimony? The whole book of Revelation is the spirit of prophecy; it is the testimony of Jesus. Very often, when we read the book of Revelation, we are so fascinated by all these events that are foretold. Every chapter is interesting and fascinating. As we enter into all these events and all these wonderful prophecies, we are locked in the forest. We are so attracted by all these prophecies, how this is the fulfillment of that, and we can become so involved. But this is not the purpose of the book of Revelation; the book of Revelation is the revelation of Jesus Christ. The spirit of prophecy is the testimony of Jesus. What is the testimony of Jesus? The testimony of Jesus is: "Jesus is Lord!" This is the testimony of Jesus.

Jesus is His earthly name, a name that He put upon Himself in His days of humiliation. The world says, "Who is this Jesus? We do not know Him. We have never heard of Him. Who is this Jesus of Nazareth?" God says, "Jesus is Lord." Jesus is Lord, and God has made Him Christ and Lord over all things. The Jesus that we preach is the Lord of all. This is the testimony of Jesus. Here you find a people who trust in the blood of the Lamb. They do not come to a point of spiritual superiority in the sense of, "I am holier than thou." They do not come to a point of thinking they are somebodies, high up with achievements. No! The blood of the Lamb is their plea; humility. They know their place before God. Yet on the other hand, they do testify that Jesus is Lord. To them there is no Lord but Jesus Christ. Jesus is Lord and Lord alone. They are completely under the authority of the Lord Jesus. Their whole life is subjected to the authority of the Lord Jesus. They are not just saying it, but their life testifies to it. They have seen and heard and experienced the Lordship of Christ. And because they have experienced it in their lives, therefore they are not ashamed to say, "Jesus is Lord." It becomes word; it becomes their testimony.

Sometimes we mix up timidity with humility. We think that we are humble, yet actually we are timid. The overcomers are not timid at all, yet it does not mean that they are arrogant. They are bold but humble. They are not afraid to testify that Jesus is Lord. And very often the conflict that enters into our lives actually revolves around this testimony of whether Jesus is Lord or not, whether Jesus is your Lord or not. Sometimes the powers of darkness will press upon you trying to so oppress you and bring you down to the point to think that Jesus is no longer Lord, and it is out of His control. Do you have such experience? Very often, you may think that things have gotten out of His hand, not only my hand but His hand, and when you come to that point your whole faith shatters. Therefore, when you are in such intense conflict, sometimes you have to shout: "Jesus is Lord!" And the enemy is routed. I do not mean to say that we should use vain repetition. It is only when you are in intense conflict, and the conflict is over this question of whether Jesus is Lord. The word of your testimony does affect the unseen world. It is a shout of faith!

They Overcome by not
Loving Their Life unto Death

Thirdly, they overcome because "they loved not their life even unto death." Hebrews tells us that Satan who has the power of death holds people in his hand because throughout their lives they are afraid to die. Death is the last enemy and is the strongest weapon of Satan. How he threatens us often with death: "If you follow the Lord, if you do not have this thing you will die. Your soul-life will suffer. Your soul-life will be reduced to poverty. You will not be satisfied, and you will die." And because Satan uses death to frighten people we are kept under bondage. But by the grace of God here is a people who are not afraid to die. They love not their life even unto death, but on the other hand, they are willing to die.

In II Corinthians 4:10 it says, "Always bearing about in the body the dying of Jesus, that the life also of Jesus may be manifested in our body." Are we willing to give up our life? The natural life must die. The natural emotional life must die. The Word of God is not dead; your emotional life should not be nourished. I mean the natural one. The Word of God says, "It must die." It is only when it goes to death that out of death the resurrection life of our Lord Jesus is manifested. I do not mean to say that you have no more emotion, but I will say you have more sure emotion, even that of our Lord.

The same thing is true with our mental life. How we are full of thoughts and opinions! How we are all counselors, not only of men but of God. How we offer our counsels so freely without being asked. And how we are hurt when our opinion is not carried out, is not obeyed. Are you willing to die to your opinion? Are you willing to die to your many thoughts and imaginations? Are you willing to die to that which you think is the most logical thing in the world? They loved not their life. The Lord said, "He that loses his life for My sake shall gain it to eternity." On the other hand, "he that gains his life," it seems as if you have gained, but the Lord says, "You lose it. You are the losers; you do not gain.

Satan is Defeated

So here is the man child. As this man child is developing within the womb of the woman, as there is the travailing and the groaning in the spirit, as there is groaning and pressure, life is enlarged. This life is growing into maturity, and as this life grows into maturity it overcomes. The battle is over life and death. Satan uses death as his conqueror, but God raises up a man child which is life full-grown, and as life is matured Satan is defeated. This is the work of the overcomers.

Dear brothers and sisters, may I emphasize again, our eyes are always looking to the things that can be seen. If we can sweep the nation, then we are overcomers. If we can do great things for God then we are overcomers, but you do not find that here. It is just this steady, silent growth of the life of Christ in the church that is being developed and growing through adversities and tribulations, a growing in understanding of the blood of the Lamb, a growing into the word of their testimony, a growing of giving away life unto resurrection, and it is when this life is precipitated, the work is done. It is not a work; it is the fruit of a life. As this man child is born, he is immediately taken to the throne and to the Lamb. But remember one thing: as the man child goes to heaven, as it were, he has to go through the air which is the base and headquarters of Satan.

When God created the earth, as we find in Genesis 1, the second day was the dividing of the waters. God did not say it is good because the air is the dwelling place of the evil powers. He is the ruler of the air according to Ephesians 2:2. But this man child is of such spiritual ascendency that he can penetrate the enemy's camp and go through it up to the throne. That is victory!

"What is man that thou are mindful of him, or the Son of man that thou has visited Him? Thou has made Him a little lower than the angels; thou has crowned Him with glory and honor" (Hebrews 2:6). This is not only fulfilled in Christ, the Overcomer, but this is fulfilled in the overcomers in union with Christ. These are men a little lower than angels, and yet spiritually, morally, they have reached such a superiority that the enemy cannot hold them. They go through the air into heaven, and because of that there is war in the air. Michael and his angels war against Satan and his followers, and there is no more place for Satan in the air. He is cast down upon the earth. Do you know what it means? His man child is the vanguard of the Lord's army. They prepare the return of the Lord because the Lord shall descend from heaven into the air, and we shall all be caught up to meet Him in the air. So the air has to be cleansed, cleared, and this is done by the male child.

Is it a small thing that the church today is in such travail? The church today has come to a point that either she goes forth or she dies. The eye of God as well as the eye of Satan is upon the male child, the overcomers at the end. And no wonder, when this male child is born then the cry goes out: "Now is come the salvation and the power and the kingdom of our God and the authority of His Christ." Through the overcomers the kingdom of God is brought from heaven to earth. The authority of Christ is to be publicly manifested upon the whole earth. May the Lord be gracious to us. We are living in the end days, and this is what is happening today. Are we among those who overcome by reason of the blood of the Lamb, by reason of the word of our testimony, and we love not our life even unto death?

Let us pray:

> Our heavenly Father, we do pray that we may get out of interpretation and get in touch with reality. In these end days Thou will have a people to maintain the testimony of Jesus. Oh Lord, our cry unto Thee is that the travail may not be in vain, that it may bring forth a male child who will be an instrument in Thy hand to bring back the King. Oh Lord, we do offer ourselves to Thee for Thy further working in our lives. We ask in the precious name of our Lord Jesus. Amen.

5—The Overcomers and the Church

Our heavenly Father, we do praise and thank Thee that we can gather again in the name of Thy beloved Son, our Lord Jesus Christ. We do desire to give Him all the glory and the power and the dominion and the love and adoration of our hearts. Our heavenly Father, we do desire that Christ may be exalted in our midst, that He may be glorified among His own people. How we praise and thank Thee, oh Lord, that thou does love Thy church and gave Thyself for it. How we praise and thank Thee for Thy care and Thy concern. Thou does say, "I will build my church upon this rock, and the gates of Hades shall not prevail against it." Oh Lord, how we praise and worship Thee. We do pray that as we gather in Thy presence that once again Thou will open Thy Word to us and open our hearts to Thy Word that it may not be just something to be heard and to be told, but it may be something wrought into our very being, our very life. Oh Lord, we do desire to create Thy refreshing in Thy church, in the life of Thy people together. We commit this time into Thy hand. Thou does know that without Thee we can do nothing, but with Thee all things are possible. We ask in Thy precious name. Amen.

The book of Revelation is a picture book. I do not know if we ever reach a time when we do not enjoy picture books. I have always liked to read picture books, and the book of Revelation is a book of pictures. We have been seeing beautiful pictures one after another, and God willing for this time we would like to see more.

Revelation 14 is a very rich chapter full of pictures, but for this time we will limit ourselves to just two pictures.

Revelation 14:1-5, 14-16—And I saw, and behold, the Lamb standing upon mount Zion, and with him a hundred and forty-four thousand, having his name and the name of his Father written upon their foreheads. And I heard a voice out of the heaven as a voice of many waters, and as a voice of great thunder. And the voice which I heard was as of harp-singers harping with their harps; and they sing a new song before the throne, and before the four living creatures and the elders. And no one could learn that song save the hundred and forty-four thousand who were bought from the earth. These are they who have not been defiled with women, for they are virgins: these are they who follow the Lamb wheresoever it goes. These have been bought from men as first-fruits to God and to the Lamb: and in their mouths was no lie found; for they are blameless...And I saw, and behold, a white cloud, and on the cloud one sitting like the Son of man, having upon his head a golden crown, and in his hand a sharp sickle. And another angel came out of the temple, crying with a loud voice to him that sat on the cloud, Send thy sickle and reap; for the hour of reaping is come, for the harvest of the earth is dried. And he that sat on the cloud put his sickle on the earth, and the earth was reaped.

Two Groups of Overcomers

There are two beautiful pictures in these two passages of Scripture. The first picture is the Lamb on Mount Zion with a hundred and forty-four thousand gathering around Him, all sealed with the name of the Father and the Lamb upon their foreheads, and they are singing a new song.

Then there is another beautiful picture beginning in verse 14. It is One like the Son of man sitting on a white cloud with a sharp sickle in his hand, and the voice came from heaven saying, "The time has come," and he throws down the sickle and reaps the harvest.

I do not believe we can mix up this hundred and forty-four thousand with the hundred and forty-four thousand in chapter 7 of the book of Revelation. We know that this number is mentioned in two places. In chapter 7 there is a hundred and forty-four thousand being sealed and in chapter 14 there is another hundred and forty-four thousand having the name of the Father and of the Lamb on their foreheads. However, these are not the same.

Now you have to excuse me again for my little interpretation. Again I hope by the end of this hour you will forget all the interpretations and enter into the reality of it. So do not quarrel with me over the interpretation; this is transient. What is important is the reality, and if you can get the reality, afterwards you can interpret it any way you like. So bear with me for a little interpretation.

As you read carefully chapter 7 and chapter 14 concerning these two groups of a hundred and forty-four thousand, within them there are enough differences to convince us that they are not one group but two different groups. For instance, in chapter 7 the hundred and forty-four thousand are sealed out of the twelve tribes of Israel. In other words, they are the faithful remnant of the nation of Israel. Whereas in chapter 14 those that are sealed are gathered out of the earth. In other words, they are gathered out of mankind in general and not Israel. Those that are sealed in chapter 7 are sealed with the seal of the living God, and the Lamb is not mentioned.

However, in chapter 14 the name of the Father and the name of the Lamb are written on the foreheads of this hundred and forty-four thousand. Immediately, you will notice the difference, for one is the seal of the living God, the Creator, and the other is the Father and the Lamb. The first group of one hundred and forty-four thousand are sealed on earth because the four winds are being held back. Before the winds begin to blow and bring destruction to the earth, these hundred and forty-four thousand are being sealed so that they may be protected from hurt and harm. In chapter 14 those who are sealed are on Mount Zion, and I think by now we ought to know what Mount Zion represents. Those that are sealed in chapter 7 are sealed before trouble begins in order that they may be kept through the trouble, but in chapter 14 those that are sealed have already gone through the trouble; they are on the other end of it. Those that are sealed in chapter 7 are in between the 6th and 7th seal, but those on Mount Zion are already high up. So by comparing these two places we discover sufficient differences to show that they are two entirely different groups. So let us turn our attention to this second group of hundred and forty-four thousand.

The Group on Mount Zion

Ones in the Fullness of Christ

First, they are on Mount Zion. Of course, we know that this Mount Zion does not mean Mount Zion literally which is in Jerusalem. When these who are on Mount Zion begin to sing, the voices come out of heaven. In other words, this is the heavenly Mount Zion, heaven itself, the seat of authority, the fullness of Christ. These hundred and forty-four thousand have entered into the fullness of Christ. Is not this what God has in mind for His own church? In Ephesians 1:23 it says, "… the church which is the body of Christ, the fullness of Him who fills all and in all." It is the will of God that His church shall be filled with the fullness of Christ. The church is the fullness of Christ because it has experienced Christ in all His fullness; that is Mount Zion. However, the hundred and forty-four thousand here have already arrived on Mount Zion, and they are there in the fullness of Christ.

The Name of the Father
and Lamb on their Foreheads

Second, they have upon their foreheads the names of the Father and the Lamb. If you put a name upon your forehead, everybody will notice it because that is the most prominent place. Of course, we know it may carry a different meaning. However, I think there is at least one meaning here. These hundred and forty-four thousand with the name of the Father and the Lamb upon their foreheads have confessed the Lord while on earth in spite of all their troubles and difficulties. Therefore, they are publicly acknowledged by the Father and by our Lord Jesus. They are being recognized by the Father: "If you confess me before men My Father will confess you before the holy angels" (see Luke 12:8). And here you find these hundred and forty-four thousand are being publically endorsed, publically claimed. God says, "Look at these people; they are Mine. I acknowledge them as Mine." God is not ashamed of them but publically recognizes these people. The prayer of Paul is that he may not be ashamed, that the Lord will not be ashamed of him (see II Timothy 1:8). That is the one passion in his heart. Here the Lord is not ashamed to acknowledge these people as His, as belonging to Him.

They are Singing a New Song

Third, they are playing on harps and singing a new song. None can understand, none can learn these songs except these hundred and forty-four thousand. We know that a harp is an instrument, and when you play a song on a harp, it is as if you are striking the cords of your heart. In playing a trumpet or playing other instruments, you may just play it, but when a harp is played your heart must be involved. In other words, it is a heart instrument. The music that comes out of the harp is the music of your heart. As they are playing on the harp, they are singing a new song. The peculiar mark of this new song is that none can learn it except these hundred and forty-four thousand. Why?

If we are musical we think we can learn any composition even though some compositions may be very difficult. But if we have a musical ear or musical talent, certainly we can learn it. But here is a song that none can learn but those who have gone through it. Actually, this is the real meaning of the song; it must come from the heart. It must be the project of our heart experience. These hundred and forty-four thousand are not shallow believers. They have gone through a lot, and as they go through these experiences with the Lord Jesus, they come out with a new song, and this is how the heavenly song is always composed. They sing a new song.

They have been Purchased Out of the Earth

Forth, they have been purchased out of the earth. Out of every tribe and tongue and nation and people, God has purchased them unto Himself.

They have not been Defiled with Women

Fifth, "These are they who have not been defiled with women, for they are virgins." I do not know how you interpret this, but personally, I do not think you can take this verse literally because if you do then celibacy really has a virtue before God. It does not seem to fit in with all the other spiritual qualifications. So personally, I would interpret it with a spiritual meaning.

You remember in II Corinthians 11 Paul said, "For I am jealous as to you with a jealousy which is of God; for I have espoused you unto one man, to present you a chaste virgin to Christ. But I fear lest by any means, as the serpent deceived Eve by his craft, so your thoughts should be corrupted from simplicity as to the Christ."

Now we know that as we believe in the Lord Jesus we are all as virgins espoused to Christ. One day He will return which will be the day of that marriage, but so far as now is concerned all believers are considered as virgins before God. These hundred and forty-four thousand remain virgins before God. They have not been defiled. They have not been beguiled. They have not been deceived from that simplicity which is in Christ Jesus.

Dear brothers and sisters, we are living at a time that is full of deception of all kinds which have only one purpose, and that is to lead us away from the simplicity of Christ. We are getting more and more complicated and more and more mysterious. There is a lack among the Lord's people of that simplicity towards Christ, that singleness of heart, that life relationship with the Lord, of not being led away by many thoughts, imaginations, and strongholds. The serpent threw a thought to Eve: "Is it true that God does not allow you to eat any of the fruit?" It was just a thought. How often we are beguiled by many thoughts and imaginations which will lead us away from that simplicity towards Christ. We are easily defiled by many things. However, these hundred and forty-four thousand are as virgins; they have not been defiled. They have been faithful to the Lord. They do not listen to many voices but hold on to the simplicity that is in Christ.

They Follow the Lamb wherever He goes

Sixth, "These are they who follow the Lamb wheresoever He goes." I like this phrase very much. They follow the Lamb wheresoever He goes. Do we follow the Lamb? Do we follow the Lamb wheresoever He goes? Do you know where He goes? He goes the way of the cross, and the hundred and forty-four thousand follow the Lamb wheresoever He goes. They do not follow their own direction or their own way. They follow Him by letting the Lamb lead the way. And we find invariably it will be the way of the cross. It is a way that means the denying of self, the taking up of our cross daily, and following Him. It means not only taking up the cross but being crucified on the cross, done away with. It is very easy to say, "I will follow the Lamb wheresoever He goes, and then He goes to an unexpected place, and immediately we say, "Lord, we did not expect that You would go there or go that far." But the hundred and forty-four thousand are completely committed to the Lamb. No matter where the Lamb goes, they go; they follow Him. These are purchased from among men to be the first-fruits unto God and unto the Lamb.

No Lie Found in their Mouths

Seventh, "And in their mouths was no lie found." We know that Satan is a liar; he is the father of all lies. The whole world lies under a big lie. How he twists the truth! How he deceives with lies! In contrast these hundred and forty-four thousand are found with no lie in their mouths. You may think that to have no lie in your mouth is a small thing, even insignificant, especially as you compare it with those who follow the Lamb whithersoever He goes, which we tend to think is something greater. It seems to be a small thing and insignificant that no lie is found in their mouth, but look into your own life, your heart, that which your mouth utters. The opposite of lie is truth, and truth is reality. Out of their mouths no lie was found. In other words, they are faithful and true witnesses of God and of His Christ. They speak what they have seen and heard and experienced. They speak the truth in love. They do not try to say one thing and mean another. They do not try to be men-pleasers. They speak the truth in love. In other words, they are real; even in their speech they are real. It is very difficult to find a real man on this earth. The whole world is a lie; the whole system is a lie, and we are living in that system. The older we grow, the cleverer we become, and we learn how to pretend. We know how to cover up. We know how to maneuver. We know how to be diplomatic, to say one thing and mean something else or say lots of words and mean nothing. We become very clever. This is found in the society of the whole world. You cannot afford to be real, for if you become real you are a fool. It is very difficult to meet a real person, but before God this is a very important characteristic. Unless we are real, we cannot be spiritual. And the consummation of realness is to be real with your mouth. So these hundred and forty-four thousand are very real. They do not live in falsehood, in pretension. They are very real people and have become real and true witnesses of Christ.

They are without Blame

Eighth, "They are without blame." Who is without blame? Our Lord Jesus. You remember in Hebrews 9 it says that He offered Himself by the eternal Spirit to God as a sacrifice without blemish (see v. 14). He is the One who has no blemish, nothing in Him to be blamed, perfect, a perfect sacrifice. He is perfect! Wonderful! But here are the hundred and forty-four thousand who are proclaimed by God to be perfect without blemish. This is the will of God. In Ephesians 1:4 it says, "According as he has chosen us in him before the world's foundation, that we should be holy and blameless before him in love." God has chosen us before the foundation of the world, and His purpose is that we should be holy and without blemish before Him. There is to be no blemish, no spot, no wrinkle, or any of such things, but we are to be perfect without blemish before God.

How can we be without blemish before God? And you know the little phrase, "in love." We will be presented before God as holy and without blemish in love. It is love that covers many things. It is love that makes us holy and without blemish.

In Ephesians 5:25b-27: "The Lord Jesus also loved the assembly, and has delivered himself up for it, in order that he might sanctify it, purifying it by the washing of water by the word, that he might present the assembly to himself glorious, having no spot, or wrinkle, or any of such things; but that it might be holy and blameless."

How can we be without blame? It all begins and ends with His love. He loved the church and gave Himself for it. He washes us with the washing of the water with the Word. In other words, His life within us is like the water that washes us together with the Word of God. We are being washed daily until we are considered as holy and without blame before Him. It is like the sacrifice that was without blemish which then could be sacrificed to God.

Who are These Wonderful People?

After having seen all these descriptions of the hundred and forty-four thousand, now we wonder who they are. They are such a wonderful people and so privileged. Now who are they? I do not pretend to

know who they are. I can only say this. In Revelation
7 we find a countless crowd standing before the
throne and before the Lamb. This represents the
overcomers of the church throughout the twenty
centuries. Now when we come to the very
consummation, it is as if God has taken out of that
countless crowd a special group to be the specimen of
the overcomers. In other words, I wonder if this
represents the elite of the overcomers. Even among
the overcomers there are degrees; some may rule ten
cities, and some five cities. The glory of this star is
different from the glory of that star. I wonder (I am
just wondering aloud) whether this hundred and
forty-four thousand represent the full thought of God
concerning the overcomers of the church.

I do not know whether this hundred and forty-
four thousand means the exact number literally or
whether they have just been given a round number to
show the multiple of twelve. I only know that the
Lord seems to pick out a round number of people to
show us that which answers fully to Himself. As you
read this description of the hundred and forty-four
thousand you find that they answer fully to Christ.
They stand with the Lamb; they are one with the
Lamb; they go wherever the Lamb goes; they are
joined to the Lamb as one. The Lamb-character
characterizes them, and this is what the overcomer
means. It is the full thought of God concerning the
overcomers.

First-Fruits to God

"These have been bought from men as first-fruits to God and to the Lamb" (4b). Who are these hundred and forty-four thousand? They are the first-fruits of the church. Does that give us some idea? You remember in Exodus 23:19 it says, "The first of the first-fruits of the land thou shalt bring into the house of Jehovah Thy God." In Leviticus 23 we find the same thing. God told Moses to tell the people that after they had entered into the land and they began to harvest, they must bring a seed of the first-fruits to the priest to be presented to God before they can eat any of the produce of the land so that they may be accepted by God. Then in Deuteronomy 26 when they presented the first-fruit to God, it is a very touching scene.

Deuteronomy 26:1-11: "And it shall be when thou comest into the land that Jehovah thy God giveth thee for an inheritance, and possesses it, and dwellest therein, that thou shall take of the first of all the fruit of the ground, which thou shalt bring of thy land which Jehovah thy God giveth thee, and shalt put it in a basket, and shalt go unto the place that Jehovah thy God will choose to cause his name to dwell there; and thou shalt come unto the priest that shall be in those days, and say unto him, I profess this day unto Jehovah thy God, that I am come unto the land that Jehovah swore unto our fathers to give us.

And the priest shall take the basket out of thy hand, and set it down before the altar of Jehovah thy God. And thou shalt speak and say before Jehovah thy God, A perishing Aramaean was my father, and he went down to Egypt with a few, and sojourned there, and became there a nation, great, mighty, and populous. And the Egyptians evil-entreated us, and afflicted us, and laid upon us hard bondage; and we cried to Jehovah, the God of our fathers, and Jehovah heard our voice, and looked on our affliction, and our labour, and our oppression; and Jehovah brought us forth out of Egypt with a powerful hand, and with a stretched-out arm, and with great terribleness, and with signs, and with wonders; and he hath brought us into this place, and hath given us this land, a land flowing with mild and honey! And now, behold, I have brought the first of the fruits of the land, which thou, Jehovah, hast given me. And thou shalt set it down before Jehovah thy God, and worship before Jehovah thy God. And thou shalt rejoice in all the good that Jehovah thy God hath given to thee, and to thy house, thou, and the Levite, and the stranger that is in thy midst."

It is a very, very touching scene. As the Israelites brought their first-fruits to God, they prayed, "Our Father was a Syrian sojourning in Egypt, and almost perished, but God has brought us out of bondage, and has brought us into this Promised Land, and here is the produce. We acknowledge that it has been given to us by God, and now we give it back to Him," and then they worshipped God. This is the meaning of the first-fruits.

If we know anything about agriculture, we know that when you cultivate a field, say a field of wheat, usually there will be a patch of wheat in this field being ripened first. Somehow this little portion seems to be able to absorb more sunshine, more nutrition. They are ripe before the rest of the wheat. They dried up first, so they are loosened from the earth first. This is the first fruits of the field, and usually the first-fruits are the best. But the Israelites do not eat the first-fruits. When they gather up these first-fruits, they bring them and offer them to God and say, "Lord, this is Yours." That is the first-fruits.

Dear brothers and sisters, here in Revelation 14 these overcomers of the church are the first-fruits in the church. The church is like a field of wheat. All the children of God are born from above; there is no difference in the life that each possesses. The only difference is when they ripen, and those who ripen first are the best. It is not a difference of kind, only a difference of degree. So these are the first-fruits.

Who are the overcomers? The overcomers, in one sense, are no different from the rest of the children of God. The life which they received is the same life that the others have received. They share the same life, they are in the same field, but somehow they dry up and get yellow first. They get matured first. Well, you may interpret it in different ways. You may say, "The sun represents the Son of righteousness, our Lord Jesus. Somehow they receive more grace, not that God is partial, but somehow they receive more grace, and they get yellow first. Or you may say that the sun represents the tribulation of this world just like the virgin in the Song of Solomon who said, "Do not look down upon me because I am black; the sun has scorched me." Maybe they get ripened through tribulations, I do not know. Nevertheless, some in the church, whether they go through tribulation or whether somehow they enjoy more of the grace of Christ, they are ready first, they are ripened first, they are loosened first.

When wheat is ripe, the roots barely touch the soil. You just lift it and harvest it. In other words, these overcomers are in the world, and yet not of the world; they just barely touch it. Thus they are ripened before God, and the first-fruits are the best. But do you think that the best is to be enjoyed by yourself? No; the best is to be presented to God in the temple; it is for God.

Probably we have a natural concept concerning overcomers. Maybe our concept is that if I am an overcomer then there will be great enjoyment for me. Well, it is true that the Lord said, "Come into the joy of the Lord." That is true, but basically, to be an overcomer is not to enjoy yourself. To be an overcomer is to let God enjoy you. That is the

116

meaning of an overcomer. Do you think that enduring through all these tribulations, following the Lamb in the way of the cross, and being strictly disciplined by the Spirit of God that one day you will have great enjoyment? You will, but this is not the motive behind it. The motive behind an overcomer is that he may be a sacrifice and offering to God. We know that no sacrifice can be offered if there is any blemish, but here they are without blemish. What is their purpose? That they may stand up and say, "Look, how perfect I am." No, that they may be offered on the altar, burned, consumed, and disappear.

Are you willing to be an overcomer? There is not much in it for you, but there is much for God. This is the meaning of overcomers. They do not have a mercenary, bargaining spirit when it comes to this matter of overcomers. I know it because it is in me. I know that sometimes there is a bargaining spirit in me just like Peter when he said, "What will we have? We have given up everything for you; now what will we have?" That is a bargaining spirit. That is not the right spirit of an overcomer. The Lord said, "You will have a hundred fold with persecution and life eternal in the age to come." The right spirit of an overcomer is that we may be for God, for His satisfaction, and for His enjoyment. If we are consumed and disappear, thank God, He is satisfied. There is nothing for ourselves; it is for Him.

The Harvest

The first-fruits guarantee the coming of the harvest. If you do not have the first-fruits, you will never have a harvest; that is for sure. But when a farmer gathers the first fruits, he knows for sure that the harvest will come; it guarantees the harvest. What is the function of the overcomers? The function of the overcomers is that because they have been matured they bring the church into maturity.

Many years ago, I was puzzled by Ephesians chapter 4:13-15 which says, "Until we all arrive at the unity of the faith and of the knowledge of the Son of God, at the full-grown man, at the measure of the stature of the fullness of the Christ; in order that we may be no longer babes, tossed and carried about by every wind of that teaching which is in the sleight of men, in unprincipled cunning with a view to systematized error; but, holding the truth in love, we may grow up to him in all things, who is the head, the Christ."

I was puzzled with this for a long time. How can the church ever arrive at this place? How can the church of God ever come to that unity of the faith and of the knowledge of the Son of God unto that full-grown man, the fullness of the stature of Christ? How can the church ever come to that? The more I looked at the condition of the church around me, the more I looked into myself, the more I became disappointed. I was reduced to despair. I said, "It can never, never arrive," as if the closer the return of the Lord seems to be, the farther away the church is from that maturity. I did not understand how it could ever be fulfilled. If the return of the Bridegroom waits for the maturity of the bride, He will never return. The bride never matures; it is an old baby. I do not know if you have the same problem.

I thank the Lord for our brother Watchman Nee. He explained it to me, and I am satisfied. I do not know if you will be satisfied, but I am satisfied with his explanation. He said, "Brother, this arriving at the fullness of Christ is to be accomplished in the overcomers of the church. When the overcomers of the church have reached the maturity of a man child being born, God considers that the whole church is ready for Him. I do not know if you agree, but I am satisfied, and the Lord seems to comfort me with this. When you have the first-fruits, then the harvest is secure. The work of the overcomers is not for themselves; the overcomers are for the whole church. Do not think that we become overcomers and then leave the church behind. Or we are overcomers, and we are to enjoy the Lord. Not so! Not so! The very maturing of the overcomers is for the maturity of the whole church; it guarantees the harvest. This is the first picture, the first preview.

Then in the latter part of this chapter the harvest comes. The apostle John saw another vision of the

Son of man sitting on a white cloud. He was not on Mount Zion, but on a white cloud with a golden crown on His head; He is the King of kings and the Lord of all. And in His hand is a sharp sickle, but He waits until another angel comes out from the temple and says, "Now the time is ready; throw down the sickle and harvest the harvest." The Lord Jesus said, "No one knows the time but the Father." When the Father says, "The time is right," the sickle is cast on the earth, and the harvest is harvested.

The Return of the Lord

In the book of Acts chapter 1 the Lord Jesus led His disciples to the mount of ascension, and after He had spoken to them He was taken up. They were all looking at Him as He was being taken up, and then a cloud took Him away; they could not see Him anymore. But they were still looking, and two men in white appeared and said, "Men of Galilee, why are you looking up? The One who has been taken up will return in like manner." When the Lord was taken up, it was in two parts. The first part was from the mount up to the cloud; He could be seen, visible. Then He was taken away by the cloud up to heaven, unseen, invisible. In like manner He shall come back. He shall come back first from the throne to the cloud, invisible. Then He shall come from the cloud to the earth and be seen by everyone. The Lamb on Mount Zion is now the Son of man sitting on a white cloud waiting to harvest His harvest. Do you know what that harvest is? That is the whole church.

In I Thessalonians 4 it says, "For the Lord himself, with an assembling shout, with archangel's voice and with trump of God, shall descend from heaven; and the dead in Christ shall rise first; then we, the living who remain, shall be caught up together with them in the clouds, to meet the Lord in the air; and thus we shall be always with the Lord. So encourage one another with these words."

Dear brothers and sisters, we are looking forward to the return of our Lord, but when He returns, He must have His first-fruits, and He must have His harvest. When the Israelites harvested, they enjoyed the harvest themselves. Whether you want to be the first-fruits for God's satisfaction and enjoyment or whether you want to be in the harvest for your own satisfaction and enjoyment is up to you. Here in this chapter we are shown the first-fruits and the harvest, the overcomers and the church. They are one, and they shall be the bride of the Lamb.

Shall we pray:

> Our heavenly Father, Thou are looking for the first-fruits to secure the harvest. Oh, our hearts do go out to Thee and cry that Thou may have the first-fruits. We confess that our fathers were slaves ready to perish, sojourning in Egypt under bondage and affliction, but Thou has

brought us out into the Promised Land, and we do desire to offer the first-fruits back to Thee. We acknowledge that this belongs to Thee. Thou shall be satisfied. Oh Lord, we ask Thee to fill our hearts with this desire that we may worship Thee and bring the first-fruits and lay them at Thy feet. We ask in the precious name of our Lord Jesus. Amen.

Made in the USA
Las Vegas, NV
30 August 2022